# GETTING THE
# RIGHT
# JOB

## A PERSONAL GUIDE TO DEVELOPING YOUR CAREER

**FRANK MUNSON • JOHN STERN • JANE WILLIS MAYER**

# ACKNOWLEDGMENTS

The authors and editors of this book would like to thank Dr. Felipe Thomaz, Assistant Professor of Marketing at the Darla Moore School of Business, University of South Carolina, for providing content about social media and its uses in the job search process throughout the book. We genuinely appreciate his time, talent, and commitment to this project.

Although it has been three years since the passing of our dear friend, John Stern, he is still missed in a profound way, and the contributions he made to this book are still greatly appreciated. His wisdom, intense understanding of the hiring process, and passion for students are still woven into the fabric of this project. John, you were a great man!

# INTRODUCTION

Learning and following the process as outlined in this book will ensure that you will be prepared, competitive, determined, and confident as you seek employment and the best job for you. To get the most out of this book, you should read each Birkman Method® report as referenced throughout the book, and you should complete the exercises outlined in each chapter.

## THIS WILL ALLOW YOU TO REALIZE THE FOLLOWING OUTCOMES:

- Using the Birkman Method®, you will fine-tune your plan and skills in light of your personal strengths and interests.
- You will be prepared and motivated to spend the necessary time to find the right job-fit for you.
- You will be confident and knowledgeable about the various interviewing processes used in the marketplace today.
- The right internship or job will enable you to be successful and move to the next level of your personal development.

No matter where you are in your college or professional career, the skills and insights you will gain, if you approach this process with focus and commitment, will be invaluable. They will serve you well now and in future times of career transition. You are encouraged to take the information provided in this textbook and your Birkman Method results seriously and to apply them immediately for best retention and results.

HTTPS://MY.BIRKMAN.COM/Q/7BBFFC75-23EE-3ED4-8296-666F589E933A

# BE INTENTIONAL

- KEEP AN OPEN MIND.
- KEEP LEARNING EVERY DAY.
- ENTERTAIN NEW IDEAS.
- KEEP BUILDING SELF-CONFIDENCE.

# HOW TO USE THIS RESOURCE

This book is designed to be used in tandem with the Birkman Method® questionnaire results. In order to complete the exercises in this workbook, you must complete the questionnaire prior to utilizing the workbook.

## STEPS FOR GETTING THE MOST OUT OF THIS RESOURCE

1. Using the link on the opposite page, your first step will be to complete the Birkman Method questionnaire. See below specific instructions before you begin.

2. Set aside 30-45 minutes to complete the questionnaire. It is best if you complete the questionnaire in one sitting.

3. While answering the questions, go with your first response; don't overthink your answers.

4. Once completed, follow the instructions on the screen to download and/or print your results. You will need these to complete the exercises contained in this book.

# TABLE OF CONTENTS

# CHAPTER 1

# Assessing Your State of Mind

OUTCOMES:

**I WILL BE OPEN TO LEARNING MORE ABOUT MYSELF AND EMBRACING MY STRENGTHS AND CHALLENGES.**

**I WILL REFLECT ON THE MEANING OF "WORK" TO ME, AND DEVELOP MY OWN SET OF PRIORITIES.**

## DECISION

The first step in the job search process begins within one's self. You must make the decision to personally prepare for the upcoming journey by making changes that will make possible a successful job search and/or career change. To adapt ourselves for maximum career fulfillment, we must change the way we personally approach challenges and adversity. This discussion harkens back to our fight or flight tendencies, and we all have unique combinations of tendencies and various ways of responding. Understanding these issues in light of a job search or career change is essential.

As described in the Introduction, this book will incorporate your unique Birkman Method® Results. You will be asked to refer to your results at points where understanding your unique tendencies is essential to working through the job search process. We will begin this process here based on the need for you to understand your basic tendencies and responses to changes and hardship. With that in mind, **please refer to the first report in your results packet, "Your Job Search" and refer to Section 2 of this report, "When the Job Search Becomes Stressful." Please read this section thoroughly before continuing.**

You can expect some or all of these emotions as you begin this process. In view of these insights, consider the following. It is all too easy to do just enough to get by. Trying to implement change

involves taking risks, and taking risks involves the possibility of failure. Too often, rather than risking failure we stay with old methods and practices. This is the safe route, but it also cuts off any possibility of advancement. Safety is the most unrewarding goal to work toward. It keeps us from learning new things and gets in the way of our reaching our true potential. We need a new attitude toward taking chances and making changes.

The more you push the boundaries of comfort, the more you will be able to take risks and make difficult decisions. An important part of risk taking is personal responsibility. You can't have one without the other. You can expect that some risks will pay off, but you must also expect some to fail. When you take a chance and make a mistake, be accountable for your actions. Admit you made an error, and explain why you undertook the step in the first place.

Honesty and accountability are key. But there is a payoff: even when you make mistakes, you can learn from them. You can grow.

And that's the whole point of risk taking and change: ultimately, they lead to new knowledge and personal growth. Whenever change comes your way, don't ask yourself, "What can I do to cope with this and ride it out?" Ask instead, "What can I do to embrace these challenges, to learn from them, and ultimately improve myself and advance my personal vision?"

Please be aware that you do have unique strengths and tendencies that will serve you well during the job search process. Being reminded of those now will provide a strong foundation for your next steps. With that in mind, **please refer to the first report in your results packet, "Your Job Search" and refer to Section 1 of this report, "Approaching Your Job Search." Please read this section thoroughly before continuing.**

Begin now considering how you will leverage these strengths to your benefit moving forward, noting that the tendencies and characteristics listed in the Birkman report just referenced are things that come naturally to you.

The business world today offers us a host of challenges that, at times, seem to bear down and smother us. If we look challenges in the eye and see them as an opportunity for growth, learning, and improvement, we will begin changing the way we view our careers.

## EXERCISE 1

1. In light of the Birkman results shared in this section, what aspect of your personality do you believe may be your biggest obstacle in finding an internship or job?

2. Similarly, what search activities that do come naturally to you may be your biggest asset?

## ATTITUDE

We need a positive attitude toward taking chances and making changes. Pushing ourselves to make difficult choices and actively seeking change will enable us to attempt activities that we are not particularly comfortable with; the more we push the boundaries of comfort, the more we are able to take risks and make difficult decisions.

Attitude isn't something imposed upon us from the outside. It's a choice. Some people respond to an uncertain business or job climate by distancing themselves from their jobs and seeking fulfillment in sources outside their work. Their heavy emotional investment may go into hobbies and other leisure-time activities, for example. But isolating our identity and sense of spiritual well-being from our work denies a crucial fact: our jobs are a vital aspect of our lives, and each day we spend an enormous amount of our time at work.

Consider these numbers. There are 168 hours in a week. If you sleep 7 hours a night, then that leaves you with 119 hours awake. Assuming you work 40 hours per week (and most people today work far more) and must spend 2 hours each day preparing for and commuting to and from work (again, a very conservative figure), then 50 hours a week—or almost half the time you are awake—is filled with your job or job-related activities. Trying to separate personal fulfillment from your work means discarding almost half of your life and categorizing it as unfulfilling.

For our lives to be full and worthwhile, we must enjoy our work, look forward to it, and draw personal satisfaction from it. To take this one step further, we not only need to draw satisfaction from our work, we need to believe that what we do effectively leverages our strengths and interests. This does not mean making work the sole focus of life; becoming so involved in a career that we neglect family and friends is just as bad as viewing our job as nothing more than a source of income. What we need to achieve is a balance between our professional lives and our personal lives. We must adapt ourselves so that even in a business climate of uncertainty and instability, we can be comfortable and can excel in our jobs and our careers. Doing so requires that we change the way we think about work, and change the way we react to conditions of the workplace.

Depending on your work experiences, or those of your parents or other family members, you may have a skewed view of "work" in general. As you continue, it will be important that you put aside preconceived notions of "work" in order to ascertain what direction you take in light of your strengths and interests.

## EXERCISE 2

1. Describe your current attitude about the process of searching for an internship or job and/or changing careers.

## CREATIVITY

# cre·ate /krē•āt/ (verb)

Merriam-Webster dictionary defines "create" as,

1. To cause to come into existence; make, originate.  2. To cause; produce; bring about.

These definitions suggest that creative thoughts have to be original, brand new, and never before tried. How many times have you heard people say when they meet a person with a talent for writing or art, "I really envy you. I wish I were creative myself." Our standard notions of creativity are very restrictive, breaking the world up into a smaller number of creative people and a vast majority of uncreative people.

Is this division really accurate, though? Certainly, few of us are ever going to try our hand at writing a novel, painting a portrait, or creating a sculpture. But this doesn't mean that we cannot be creative. Creativity is not so much a talent as a way of thinking, which is something that can be learned and expanded. It involves the willingness to experiment and make changes, a confidence in one's own skills and capabilities, and the ability to adapt useful ideas to his or her own circumstances.

Let's look a little closer at the last dictionary definition of creativity. If we accepted it literally, then we would believe that we couldn't be creative unless we were doing things and thinking thoughts that no one has ever come up with before. But there is no writer, painter, musician, or any other artist who doesn't have models and masters from whom they have learned their techniques and received inspiration. The early work of virtually every great novelist and poet is highly imitative of the writers they admire. Only as they mature and develop do they begin to develop their own style and discover their own individual material. Some forms of art, in fact, such as the collage and digitally-sampled music, involve no original material at all. The individuality of the work—indeed the creativity—exists solely in the way in which the borrowed material is arranged and adapted.

Creativity, then, is not in the ideas and techniques we use, but rather in how we use them. Anyone can learn to be creative. We must simply look for new ideas and different ways of doing things while always taking into consideration how we can adapt those ideas for our own use.

This is easier for some than it is for others. Some individuals are wired to create and enjoy change and new ways of approaching situations, others prefer the predictable, secure methods that have been utilized in the past. As you continue to explore your Birkman Method® results throughout this book you will learn more about your natural tendencies in this area, but for now, consider the following.

Too often when we are searching for new ways of doing things, we are looking for "recipes" that we can follow step-by-step without having to modify any details. That's far easier than coming up with our own plan, but it has its dangers. Consider, for example, the countless fad diets that are printed in magazines and available online. If you want to lose weight, they claim, all you have to do is follow this simple step-by-step plan. It all sounds so easy, but these diets never really seem to work. How could they? Everyone's body is different, and one person's schedule and habits are different from another's. A single diet can't work for everyone.

The same can be said for plans and methods for improving your job search process. New books, blogs, and articles are available weekly and are loaded down with charts, graphs, plans, and techniques. No person could ever hope to implement all the plans; very few of us can fully implement our individual plan.

This is by no means to say that these available resources and plans are without merit. Oftentimes, they are filled with wonderful ideas, even though their schemes cannot work for us as a whole. Withthat in mind, it is important to approach this book with creativity, considering what the authors have to say and analyzing the ideas they are laying out. The material is adaptable and can be modified for individual needs and preferences.

Personal growth is about becoming the person we have the potential to be. A period of unemployment or time planning for a career/job change can absolutely change your life. This can be a place where gladness and hunger meet, therefore motivating you for your journey.

## EXERCISE 3

1. What do you need to do to personally prepare yourself for the journey to come?

2. What do you hope to gain from this book/class/seminar?

# BE INTENTIONAL

- DON'T TRY TO CHANGE ANYBODY BUT YOURSELF.
- WE CAN ALL LEARN FROM ONE ANOTHER.
- BE COMMITTED TO EXCELLENCE, HIGH STANDARDS, AND CONTINUING IMPROVEMENT.
- THE SCIENTIFIC METHOD OF LEARNING: CONFRONTATION, SEARCH, TRYOUT, AND EVALUATION IS A GREAT PROCESS FOR DEVELOPMENT.

# CHAPTER 2
# What Motivates You in the Workplace?

OUTCOME:

**I WILL LEARN WHAT MOTIVATES ME PERSONALLY AND PROFESSIONALLY IN ORDER TO UNDERSTAND WHAT CAREER AND WORK ENVIRONMENTS BEST SUIT ME.**

## UNDERSTANDING MOTIVATION

To motivate means to provide with an incentive or motive. Why do you need to know and be able to document what motivates you? Because according to a study conducted by the consulting firm Towers Perrin, which surveyed almost 90,000 workers in 19 countries, only 21% of workers are "engaged" in their jobs. "Engaged" is human resources jargon for being ready to expend some extra effort at work. Engagement is the degree to which workers connect to the job or company emotionally, are aware of what they need to do to add value, and are willing to take that action.

To be engaged, you must be motivated, and motivation is typically highest when the job offers an opportunity to learn, develop new skills, and acquire and demonstrate competence. Managers cannot get us motivated to achieve! They can help us look for opportunities to achieve and they can help build an environment that is conducive to achievement, but each of us has to assume the responsibility for our own motivation. Think about your own motivating factors—what keeps you excited about achievement?

## EXERCISE 1

1. Select a job or internship you believe you would like to pursue, visualize what you want to achieve with it, and try to see in your mind that success happening at a specific time and place.

2. Now, make a written list of your motivating factors by answering this question: "What made you happy and proud at the time you visualized your success?"

Most managers and companies think that money in salary and veritable pay programs are the main motivators. Once a person's basic money needs are met, then only approximately 25% of workers are motivated by money. Listed below are some possible "individual motivating factors":

- SENSE OF ACCOMPLISHMENT
- CONTRIBUTION TO OTHERS
- POTENTIAL FOR INCREASED RESPONSIBILITIES AND INCOME
- VISION
- BELIEFS
- PERSONAL ACHIEVEMENT
- PERSONAL GROWTH
- SATISFACTION / COMMITMENT TO A GOOD JOB
- RECOGNITION
- APPRECIATION
- AUTONOMY / SELF-GOVERNANCE / DESIRE TO MAKE OWN DECISIONS
- HIGH PERSONAL STANDARDS
- CURIOSITY / DESIRE TO LEARN
- PRESTIGE / POSITIVE ATTENTION
- POWER / DESIRE TO INFLUENCE PEOPLE
- ORDER / DESIRED AMOUNT OF ORGANIZATION IN DAILY LIFE
- REJECTION / FEAR OF REJECTION / FEAR OF JOB LOSS
- AVERSION TO ANXIETY AND STRESS
- LEADERSHIP
- HONOR / DESIRE TO BEHAVE IN ACCORDANCE WITH CODES OF CONDUCT
- FAMILY / DESIRE TO SPEND TIME WITH FAMILY.

This, of course, is only a partial list because we are all different. Take a moment and circle the motivators listed above you believe have the most impact on your success and satisfaction. Please do this prior to reading the remainder of this chapter.

## THE BIRKMAN METHOD® AND WORKPLACE MOTIVATION

When we are first born our needs are basic. We need food, protection, physical comfort, and sleep. Babies are very in tune with these needs and they vocalize loudly to ensure these needs are met. Overtime, our needs get more complicated, as does the process of getting those needs met. In addition, our family, society, and culture may have instilled in us the idea that we should not expect to get our needs met on a regular basis, or that our needs are not that important.

Earlier in this chapter we discussed your motivating factors in general terms by utilizing a visualization exercise. Now we will peel back one more layer and focus on some very individualized, personal needs.

In the context of this book, when conducting a search or managing a career change, your needs are extremely important. It is simply not possible to manage an effective job search process without being clearly in tune with one's needs. Job satisfaction and personal fulfillment depend upon successfully managing needs and seeking healthy ways of getting needs met on a regular basis.

At the end of the previous chapter you were asked to list and prioritize your needs. Take a moment to glance back at what you wrote. This chapter will take this process one step further. We will focus on the Birkman Method® results to come to a deeper understanding of personal needs, with a focus on work environments that are likely to meet those needs, and on the reactive behaviors that can be predicted if those needs are not met.

With that in mind, let's begin looking at some of your Birkman Method® results focusing on needs. We will look specifically at needs that relate to interpersonal and communication needs, company cultural issues, management style preferences, and general needs. To get us started, we will focus on the center of our existence: our interpersonal, or relationship needs.

## INTERPERSONAL AND COMMUNICATION NEEDS

We are relational people. All of us strive for, and long for, meaningful relationships. And even though we are not necessarily looking for these types of relationships while conducting an internship or job search, we do have to accept the fact that other people play a key role in our success or failure in this process. With this in mind, it is crucial that we understand what we inherently need from others. As a reminder, the Birkman Method's basic approach centers on understanding one's needs and the needs of others. This is the bread and butter of the instrument and its effectiveness in this process. The report you will review next provides an overarching description of your interpersonal needs and communication styles, particularly from key individuals in your life.

## EXERCISE 2

1. **Please locate and read, "How do You Prefer Others to Talk to You."** Do you feel the statements about your interpersonal needs are basically true?

2. Do you think these needs are likely to consistently be met in the job search process?

The reality is that all of our needs are rarely met all of the time. The search process is no different. It will be important for you to be aware of your personal "redflags" or reactive behaviors in these situations. These behaviors manifest when the needs in these areas are not met. They are reactionary in nature but they can be controlled. You must be able to continue moving forward in your job search without getting derailed, and knowing how you are likely to react to adversity is key.

Only through knowing and understanding these behaviors can you begin to control them.

**Please locate and read, "How You Handle Other People" - Section 2.** Can you think of any real life examples when these behaviors interfered with your ability to move forward in a situation? If so, what did you do to get past it?

You can expect these particular behaviors to appear during this process, probably more than once. Keep in mind, however, that these needs are real and matter to you. With that in mind, it will be important that you implement strategies to manage these early on in the process. Otherwise the success of your search will be impacted in a profoundly negative way. What are some strategies that you would utilize in this process? How will you manage these feelings and reactions?

## WORK ENVIRONMENT NEEDS

Most people underestimate the importance of the work environment, at least early in their careers. Honestly, most focus on what job they want, not where they want to work. This is a crucial mistake, one that we hope you will not make in your current search. To that end, this section will focus on gaining a greater understanding of your unique needs as it relates to work environment. When discussing work environment, it is important to separate an understanding of the physical environment from the social and corporate culture associated with a particular workplace. While the physical can be an important factor (indoor desk setting vs. outside or manufacturing environment) what tends to matter more to most people is the management style and "feel" of the workplace.

## EXERCISE 4

**Please locate and read, "Organizational Fit."** In light of these Birkman descriptors, please answer the following questions:

1. Have you ever worked in an environment that was clearly uncomfortable for you? If yes, what do you think made you uncomfortable?

2. Have you worked for a specific manager who did not address the basic needs described in the Organizational Fit report? If so, what could that manager have done differently to better motivate you?

Most people don't leave a job, they leave a manager. In addition, most employees do not fully understand what they need from a workplace or a manager and are unable to ask for what they need. Please make sure you are familiar with what you actually need so that you can access a job opportunity and a potential boss effectively in the future.

## GENERAL NEEDS

Throughout most of this book we will highlight specific Birkman results as they relate to the tactical aspects of the job search process. We believe, however, that it is imperative that you have a basic understanding of your general results before we continue the discussion. With that in mind, please take some time to carefully read the following and then record your reaction in the space provided.

### EXERCISE 5

1. **Please locate and read, "Some Basic Information About You."** Do you believe that this is an accurate description of you? Which aspects resonated the most?

2. To continue this train of thought, being truly open and honest with yourself, please read, "Your Possible Challenges."

## EXERCISE 6

1. Which of the behaviors listed in the Your Possible Challenges report have you seen manifest the most in your life?

2. Have they interfered in past situations, making you ineffective and/or uncomfortable? Please note: It is more important now, more than ever, that you maintain an awareness of these potential stress behaviors, monitor them, and avoid them whenever possible.

# BE INTENTIONAL

- INTEGRITY IS YOUR GREATEST STRENGTH.
- DON'T WORK FOR MONEY; WORK FOR THE OPPORTUNITY TO LEARN AND SERVE.
- ONE OF OUR PURPOSES IN LIFE IS TO BRING OUT THE BEST WITHIN OURSELVES AND OTHERS.
- MONEY IS VERY IMPORTANT, BUT WORK FOR YOUR DREAMS, BELIEFS, VALUES, AND WHAT YOU ENJOY.

# CHAPTER 3

# Perception is Reality—
# What is Your Personal Brand?

---

OUTCOME:

## I WILL BECOME MORE AWARE OF HOW I AM PERCEIVED AND HOW MY BEHAVIOR IMPACTS OTHERS.

---

Whether we like it or not, others' perceptions of us become their reality. There are certainly times when others' conclusions about our behavior, accomplishments, appearance, or personality seem unfair. It also may feel like there is nothing we can actively do to control or manage the thoughts of others. While this is true at times, there are steps we can each take to control what is called our "personal brand." While you are in an active internship or job search, maintaining a vigilant awareness of this "brand" is crucial, and an active awareness should, in reality, become part of managing your career over time.

Your "brand" is driven by your behavior and reactions, your approach to problem solving, and your interactions with others. It is also important to remember that you have a "digital" brand, thanks to the numerous social media platforms available, and to the internet in general. Both aspects of your brand will be addressed in this chapter.

## YOU ARE WHO YOU ARE, BUT...

We ended the previous chapter with some general information about you, along with some potential behavioral pitfalls that may impact your search. The pitfalls listed are what Birkman calls "stress behaviors." These are reactions to situations where one's needs are not met over time. It is extremely important that you remain aware that these behaviors may manifest during stressful times, so as to avoid or at least manage them

First, we will focus on the way you usually behave, which most people would refer to as your personality. We believe this is how you were born, and describes the basic ways you are wired. We also believe that these behaviors describe the ways you are most productive and successful. However, regardless of how "normal" your typical behaviors may feel to you, they can be misconstrued by others.

With that in mind, we will now focus on how you are perceived by others in light of and because of some of the very characteristics that make you uniquely you. Please understand that we are not proposing that anyone strive to be something they are not, or that they attempt to change their basic makeup. The purpose here is to make you aware of how some of your typical, and we might add "comfortable," behaviors are potentially viewed by others.

We will start with a look at how you are likely to "handle" other people in a work environment.

## EXERCISE 1
**Locate and read, "Understanding the Components," Section A: Components: Usual: Comments.**

1. Do these descriptors feel accurate to you?

2. If so, do you see any areas others may perceive in a negative way?

Now let's take a look at what Birkman says about the ways in which you try to influence others. Influencing others is a very important part of the search process. Your role as the potential intern or employee is to influence an employer to hire you. Understanding this aspect of who you are is crucial.

## EXERCISE 2
**Locate and read,"How You Seek to Influence Others." Focus on the first section only, "Effective Approach."**

1. Do these descriptors feel accurate to you?

2. If so, do you see any area others, particularly future managers, may perceive in a negative way?

3. How could you adapt any of these, if needed, to better serve your purpose in the search process?

Now that you have evaluated these areas in light of your usual, comfortable approach, it is important to look at these same 2 areas from the perspective of stress or reactive behaviors. During a search, the level of personal stress is high. It is very likely that you will revert to stress or reactive behaviors at least occasionally, which is why we introduced them at the end of Chapter 2. We will continue to revisit them throughout the book, but for now let's simply focus on these 2 areas.

**Please look back at, "How You Seek to Influence Others," and this time read "Less Effective Approach."**

Although none of these behaviors are very positive, do they adequately describe the ways you react when feeling stressed or pressured?

If so, which specific behaviors seem the most likely to manifest in your life?

How could they negatively impact your search and potentially derail your efforts?

Exercise 3 was probably not a fun exercise, but it is necessary in order to mentally prepare for the search process. Please remember that in your search, and ultimately on the job, you are the "product" that is for sale. Your personal "brand" is impacted by all of your behaviors—the good and the bad. If you are going to be deliberate in managing your personal brand, then you must be aware of who you really are.

## YOUR ONLINE BRAND

In discussing your personal brand it is important for you to understand that during a search process, you are the "product" being sold. Like any product, your brand is a huge differentiator, and likely the reason you would get a job or internship instead of someone else even when both of you have all of the same qualifications. Strong brands not only drive choice, but also value, meaning that a strong personal brand could also lead to higher pay. All the more reason to be mindful of your brand!

So, how does social media affect your personal brand? As it does with most things, social media multiplies the size and scope of your brand. If previously you were worried about what you said to someone, how you acted during an interview, or how you dressed/presented yourself in a more social environment, consider now the amount of information potentially available about you online. Consider your status updates and pictures on Instagram, Snapchat, Twitter, LinkedIn and Facebook, and be mindful of the things you mention that are of interest to you. Consider information that you make available about yourself, as well as the things your friends make available. There is a potentially enormous amount of information impacting your brand, most of it related to things that would never come up in a professional/interview setting.

It is true that there is an ongoing discussion about the ethics of firms using this personal information in hiring decisions, but there are largely no laws describing what can and cannot be used, only guidelines. Additionally, remember that recruiters are humans too, and are doing their best to find the best person for the job; it can be difficult to avoid looking up your candidates online. In fact, more than 70 percent of companies check their candidates' online profiles, and this number is likely to continue growing. So, the best approach is to actively manage what others can see about you. You will have a "digital footprint" simply by virtue of existing and interacting online, so you might as well make it work for you.

Some things that are not discussed in applications or interviews will be obvious from your digital presence: gender, race, ethnicity, age, any disabilities, etc. Technically, these items are legally protected, and are not to influence hiring decisions. However, other items have cost applicants their job opportunities: inappropriate photographs, bad attitudes towards previous employers and fellow employees, discriminatory comments, or general information about drug use/abuse and or excessive alcohol use. It is also not uncommon for recruiters to gauge applicants' communication skills by how they express themselves online, nor is it unlikely for them to confirm prior experience and/or qualifications through social media. Even if many of these items are not officially entered into the firm's decision criteria, there is still the "I can't un-see this picture, or that comment" which could damage your brand, and with it your chances at landing a specific position. It is possible for recruiters to simply assume that you are "not a good fit for the company's culture" and dismiss an application at that point.

However, there is a fairly straightforward solution. Start by making your social media accounts private (if able), thus limiting what information is visible outside of your group of friends/family. Additionally, manage your list of friends carefully. Privacy settings are of little use to you if you add the recruiter/interviewer to your friends list after your meeting. At no point can recruiters request your social media passwords (this is one instance where several states have passed a law protecting individuals against social media intrusion).

For those services where privacy is not an option, consider managing your content. Pay attention to what you say, what you post, and what others post about you. This is a tremendously important step as we move away from a "hiding the bad/inappropriate stuff" strategy to using social media to your advantage as a brand-building tool. How?

Make sure that the information you are providing in your public social media accounts is consistent with what you present in person, and that both of these are consistent with the professional brand/impression you are attempting to create. This is easily done via:

1. **Engaging in online conversation.** There are several groups online, specifically, within LinkedIn, that are specific for industry-related or trade-related discussions. Join the conversation to demonstrate knowledge, expertise, and interest.
2. **Sharing Content.** Engage with experts in your field and share what they have to say with others. Share interesting/relevant articles.
3. **Creating Content.** Contribute your own insights via blog posts, articles, etc.

Perception is truly reality, and social media does provide you with tools to manage perception, your image, your personal brand, and your value to potential employers. Creating a strong brand as suggested above might not only assist with current applications, but might also translate into new opportunities as more managers and recruiters come across your content.

# BE INTENTIONAL

- STAY OPEN-MINDED.
- DEMONSTRATE RESPECT FOR EVERYBODY YOU COME IN CONTACT WITH, INCLUDING THOSE WHO YOU DON'T BELIEVE HAVE ANY AUTHORITY. RECRUITERS OFTEN CONSULT WITH THESE PEOPLE (RECEPTIONISTS, ASSISTANTS, ETC.), AND THOSE YOU DON'T SEE.
- MAKE MISTAKES. LEARN FROM THEM AND ADMIT TO THEM EARLY.
- DON'T BE SARCASTIC.
- BE HONEST.

# CHAPTER 4

# Career Direction

OUTCOME:

## I WILL BECOME MORE AWARE OF MY CAREER INCLINATIONS AND WILL LEARN MORE ABOUT CURRENT JOB AND CAREER OPPORTUNITIES.

The Birkman Method® provides a great roadmap for individuals seeking to learn more about what interests them in ways that could lead to a satisfying, rewarding career. You are encouraged to spend ample time understanding your individual Birkman Career Report. This will be pivotal as you begin to see which directions may make the most sense for you. The exercises at the end of this lesson will guide you in this process.

When you completed the Birkman Assessment, you participated in an "interest" inventory where you were asked to select your preferences from a series of listed professions. The following career categories, and your respective scores, were derived from that portion of the assessment.

Please note a few things as you review this information:

1. This is NOT a measurement of skill.

2. It is a measure of interest. When given choices between specific careers, you were assessed on which professions you regularly selected and which ones you never selected.

3. Any area scored 7-10 are areas you gravitate towards and find interesting and appealing.

4. Any areas scored 4-6 are areas for which you are indifferent, meaning you don't gravitate towards or away from them.

5. Any areas scored 1-3 are areas you genuinely gravitate away from, so it is very unlikely that you would find job satisfaction or a good fit in these areas.

## YOUR BIRKMAN CAREER FOCUS REPORT

Please find and read, "Career Focus." This report is comprehensive and will take time to fully absorb. Don't rush through this reading.

## EXERCISE 1

Spend a few minutes rereading the areas where you scored 7-10. In the space below brainstorm the various jobs that could fall into these areas. After you have created the list, place a check mark next to the jobs that sound the most appealing.

## EXERCISE 2

Review the jobs you marked with a check mark in the previous exercise. Take a few minutes to rank these from "most desirable" to "least desirable" in the space provided below.

## EXERCISE 3

Finally, reread those areas in your Career Focus Report where your score was 1-3. In the space below, summarize these areas. As a reminder, these are areas that you typically gravitate away from, so it is important to be familiar with them as a reminder of what might be a stretch career choice for you.

# BE INTENTIONAL

- MANY INTERNSHIPS AND JOBS ARE FOUND THROUGH NETWORKING AND REFERRALS. GET SOMEONE'S SUPPORT.
- DECIDE WHAT YOU REALLY WANT TO DO AND BE PERSISTENT.
- TO HELP DECIDE WHAT YOU REALLY WANT TO DO, FIGURE OUT YOUR STRENGTHS AND THE SKILLS YOU ENJOY USING.
- TAKE YOUR FOOT OFF FIRST BASE. WHAT'S THE WORST THAT CAN HAPPEN? GO FOR IT!

# CHAPTER 5

# Evaluating Your Accomplishments

OUTCOMES:

**I WILL DEVELOP A FULL UNDERSTANDING OF THE TOP EIGHT COMPETENCIES EMPLOYERS VALUE BEYOND FUNCTIONAL EXPERTISE.**

**I WILL HAVE A LIST OF MY ACCOMPLISHMENTS THAT PROVIDE EVIDENCE OF MY STRENGTHS IN THE TOP COMPETENCIES DESIRED BY EMPLOYERS.**

At this point in our process you should have a better understanding of the following:

- ASPECTS OF THE JOB SEARCH THAT COULD DERAIL YOU
- THE MOTIVATING FACTORS THAT MUST BE MET IN YOUR LIFE
- THE BASIC CAREER DIRECTION THAT MAKES THE MOST SENSE FOR YOU

Now it is time to begin personalizing your actual search.

In light of the fact that employers are primarily interested in how you can add value to their organization, you must become comfortable discussing your successes, strengths, and skillsets. Why? Because these same employers are going to evaluate you by assessing how you have added value in the past.

The first thing you must do is evaluate your past successes and consider them in light of outcomes and skills. To do this, you must begin a deep evaluation of your strengths and how those strengths have had a positive impact in the past.

In addition, please be aware that there are specific strengths and abilities for which most organizations screen. These are often referred to as core competencies. You must be able to give evidence that you possess these skills and strengths if you are going to be successful in the job search.

With this in mind, and in light of the career direction information you discovered in the previous chapter, it is time to define your strengths and skills.

## IDENTIFYING AND CONFIRMING STRENGTHS

The following is an exercise designed to acquaint you with the core competencies today's employers indicate are the most important when they screen for internships or full-time positions. This exercise is also designed to help identify specific examples from your past where your strengths and skills added value to an organization or group. To get the most from this, consider what were your most professionally satisfying experiences when you were working or striving to achieve certain goals or handling specific responsibilities. This could have been in school, while working part-time or full-time, or as part of a personal project, family activity, or any group or team memberships. There may be other possibilities beyond this list. Just describe and document your experiences.

1 These core competencies are based on recent data collected by The National Association of Colleges and Employers (NACE). Find more information at http://www.naceweb.org/career-readiness/competencies/career-readiness-defined/.

**PLEASE NOTE:**

It is imperative that you complete this exercise as it lays the groundwork for building all of your marketing materials and for adequate preparation for future interviews. This will take time and it may be advisable to complete the exercise in two or three sittings.

## EXERCISE 1

### The following steps should be followed for each of the Competencies listed:

1. Examine the definition or explanation of the strength and get a feel for what it means.

2. Answer each question posed to achieve a realistic self-assessment. Please write all of your responses down in a notebook. You will need these notes in the following chapter when you begin developing your resume. This information will also be helpful later when you begin preparations for the interview process.

3. Describe in detail your past behavior that will confirm and document each competency.

### CRITICAL THINKING/PROBLEM SOLVING:

Exercise sound reasoning to analyze issues, make decisions, and overcome problems (The individual is able to obtain, interpret, and use knowledge, facts, and data in this process, and may demonstrate originality and inventiveness.)

1. Describe a situation when you used Critical Thinking and Problem Solving skills effectively.
2. What was the problem or challenge that you faced?
3. What did you specifically do to help reach a resolution?
4. What were the results or outcomes?

### TEAMWORK/COLLABORATION:

Build collaborative relationships with colleagues and customers representing diverse cultures, races, ages, genders, religions, lifestyles, and viewpoints (The individual is able to work within a team structure, and can negotiate and manage conflict.)

1. Describe a situation in which you were an effective team member.
2. What problem or challenge did the team face?
3. What role did you play on the team and is this a role you often play when working in groups?
4. What was the outcome or result?

## PROFESSIONALISM/WORK ETHIC:

Demonstrate personal accountability and effective work habits (e.g., punctuality, working productively with others, and time workload management), and understand the impact of non-verbal communication on professional work image (The individual demonstrates integrity and ethical behavior, acts responsibly with the interests of the larger community in mind, and is able to learn from his/her mistakes.)

1. Describe a situation in which your performance exceeded others' expectations.
2. What positive outcome did you achieve that benefited the organization?
3. What specific characteristic or trait of yours became evident to those around you during this experience?
4. What are some things others said about you after this experience?

## ORAL/WRITTEN COMMUNICATIONS:

Articulate thoughts and ideas clearly and effectively in written and oral forms to persons inside and outside of the organization (The individual has public speaking skills; is able to express ideas to others; and can write/edit memos, letters, and complex technical reports clearly and effectively.)

1. Describe a work- or school-related situation in which it was extremely important for you to be clearly understood.
2. Describe the ways in which you communicated that proved to be most effective (formal presentation, written document, open discussion).
3. How did you know that you were clearly understood?
4. How would you describe your communication style?

## LEADERSHIP:

Leverage the strengths of others to achieve common goals, and use interpersonal skills to coach and develop others (The individual is able to assess and manage his/her emotions and those of others; use empathetic skills to guide and motivate; and organize, prioritize, and delegate work.)

1. Describe a situation in the past when you were in a clear leadership position either formally or informally.
2. What problem or challenge were you facing in this leadership position?
3. What key words best describe your leadership style?
4. What was the outcome or result achieved?

## DIGITAL TECHNOLOGY:

Leverage existing digital technologies ethically and efficiently to solve problems, complete tasks, and accomplish goals (The individual demonstrates effective adaptability to new and emerging technologies.)

1. Describe a time when you utilized an unfamiliar technology to solve a problem.
2. What process did you go through to learn how to use this technology?
3. How, specifically, did you use the technology?
4. What was the outcome? How did the technology support a resolution?

## CAREER MANAGEMENT:

Identify and articulate one's skills, strengths, knowledge, and experiences relevant to the position desired and career goals, and identify areas necessary for professional growth (The individual is able to navigate and explore job options, understands and can take the steps necessary to pursue opportunities, and understands how to self-advocate for opportunities in the workplace.)

1. What are your greatest strengths and how can you prove this?
2. Describe a situation in which you advocated for yourself for a position or job.
3. What skills did you use to determine you had the qualifications for this position or job?
4. What did you learn about yourself through this process?

## GLOBAL/INTERCULTURAL FLUENCY:

Value, respect, and learn from diverse cultures, races, ages, genders, sexual orientations, and religions (The individual demonstrates openness, inclusiveness, sensitivity, and the ability to interact respectfully with all people and understand individuals' differences.)

1. Describe a situation in which you showed great sensitivity to differences and were truly inclusive.
2. Did you have opposition to your actions in this situation?
3. What did you learn about yourself through this experience?
4. What did you learn about others through this experience?

## EXERCISE 2

1. Prioritize or rank each competency based on your perception of your strengths.

2. Please review the eight competencies and your answers to the coinciding questions in Exercise 1. Now, rank your top five competencies here.

   a. _____

   b. _____

   c. _____

   d. _____

   e. _____

# BE INTENTIONAL

- PRACTICE TELLING YOUR STORIES AND SHARING YOUR PAST EXPERIENCES.
- COMPETENCY REQUIREMENTS IN THE WORKPLACE CHANGE OVER TIME. BE SURE TO STAY CURRENT!

# CHAPTER 6

# Creating Your Marketing Materials

OUTCOMES:

## I WILL FULLY UNDERSTAND HOW TO CREATE A RESUME STRESSING MY STRENGTHS AND SKILLS.

## I WILL DEVELOP AN UNDERSTANDING THAT I AM THE PRODUCT AND MUST BE PREPARED TO "SELL" MYSELF AS A VALUE-ADDED SOLUTION.

## ré·su·mé / (noun)

Merriam-Webster dictionary defines "ré·su·mé" as
A summary, especially a brief record of one's personal history and experience submitted with a job application.

IN REALITY, A RESUME'S PURPOSE IS TO GET AN INTERVIEW, IDEALLY FOR A DESIRED JOB, INTERNSHIP, OR POSITION THAT WILL PLAY TO ONE'S STRENGTHS AND MOTIVATIONAL FACTORS.

This is a paradigm (an example or model) shift for most people, and it impacts all aspects of the search. In today's marketplace, a resume is a sale's tool. It can and should aid you in achieving what you want by landing relevant interviews and networking opportunities. It helps you communicate in a clearer, concise, and believable manner. That said, it is important to remember that 98% of Fortune 500 companies use Applicant Tracking Systems (ATS) that incorporate artificial intelligence (AI) into the resume and applicant screening process. Because of this it is critical that your top skills and qualifications be clear on the resume.

## DEVELOPING YOUR RESUME

Consider the following BEFORE starting to work on your resume. Write down your thoughts in the same notebook you used to record your competency based accomplishments in the previous chapter. All of the information you have recorded will be used to build your resume.

## SELECT AN AREA OF FOCUS

Decide what type of job or internship you want and write it at the top of a piece of paper. Think about specific job titles as well as a general career direction. Refer back to your Career Report if needed to come up with specific titles.

## EDUCATION

List your educational qualifications. Include your degree(s) in this list and the date of your graduation or anticipated graduation.

List your total grade point averages if 3.0 or higher, or you can indicate only your major grade point average if it is 3.0 or higher.

Record any special projects or studies in which you may have taken part, such as field work, research projects, etc.

## PAST WORK EXPERIENCE

Think back through every job you have held (volunteer and paid) and detail job duties and responsibilities for each one. Try to summarize your role in two to three sentences. Write down specifics about the organization and operation including size of organization, how many employees, etc. in this section.

## ACCOMPLISHMENTS

Now, think about specific accomplishments you achieved in each job. What did you do beyond the daily expectations of the job? Refer to the notes you took in the previous chapter to remind you of specific experiences that corresponded to the core competencies outlined.

- Did you exceed sales quotas or performance goals?
- Did you save the organization money?
- Did you generate revenue?
- Did you increase efficiency or productivity?
- Did you deliver outstanding customer service?

Try to write down at least two accomplishments for each job that you can quantify or qualify in some way (see examples below). Please note these tips as you craft these statements.

- Accomplishment statements should provide evidence of your productivity and show how you added value to an organization. They briefly capture the actions you took and the results you achieved. Work to make each statement interesting so that people who read your resume will want to get more details about your accomplishments. Be sure you note any cost savings, and mention innovations, changes, or actions that show you actively produced desired results.

- Accomplishment statements should quickly communicate to employers that you can do the job. Be sure your strengths and skills come across and that everything you write down supports the job you're targeting and the strengths and skills it requires.

- If you can't answer the question "So what?" about each bullet point (meaning why/how did this action bring value to an employer?), it should be reworked to answer that question, or it should be eliminated.

## STRONG ACCOMPLISHMENT STATEMENT EXAMPLES

- Introduced a continuous improvement program that minimized waste and boosted efficiency.
- Contributed to team initiatives that increased daily productivity and reduced errors.
- Increased revenue by designing eye-catching displays and utilizing suggestive selling techniques.
- Saved 10% over previous cost for part by researching prices on the internet.
- Organized a chapter of 150 women for the recruitment of over 700 potential new members.
- Planned and implemented a thrift sale, raising over $3000 for Juvenile Diabetes.
- Documented daily water safety records accurately 100% of the time.
- Created and managed daily rotation for seven lifeguards to maintain safety for swimmers.

## POOR ACCOMPLISHMENT STATEMENT EXAMPLES

- Responsibilities included implementation of policies and procedures. Trained new employees, interfaced with subordinates and vendors and light correspondence.
- Responsible for cleaning and straightening up clothes racks at closing time.
- Dealt with customer service issues. Various sales activities.
- Assisted the public with their questions and concerns.

## COMMUNITY ACTIVITIES

Write down any of your activities that were not associated with attendance at a school. Examples would include scouting, fundraisers, civic activities, community-sponsored athletic programs, etc. Again, think not just in terms of membership, but rather the roles you played and the accomplis ments you achieved.

**EXAMPLE:**

Organized a car wash that raised over $2000 for the community food bank.

## LEADERSHIP ACTIVITIES

Write down any and all activities in which you participated. For example, if you are in a fraternity or an honorary organization and you have held a leadership position, make certain that you write down your role(s) in addition to your membership(s). Describe what you did in each membership/role.

## HONORS AND AWARDS

List honors and awards you have received including scholarships, athletic awards, academic awards, etc. Describe the reasons you received each honor or award.

## GENERAL GUIDELINES

Before you begin the draft process, please read the following caveats, warnings, and snippets of advice from various professionals and employers. Please keep these in mind as you create your first draft. Begin each sentence with strong action verbs like planned, organized, and directed. Make sentences positive, brief, and accurate.

- Misspelled or misused words reveal careless work habits and laziness. Double and triple check every time you revise your document! Do the final check on a hard copy and not on the computer.

- Employers want specifics on what you can do for them, NOT information about what you want from the job.

- Everywhere and always, if you describe the duties you perform and don't include your accomplishments, your resume is virtually assured of a near-death experience.

- A resume isn't your biography. Employers want to know "what have you done lately?" In other words, what have you done while in college and maybe in high school.

- Wherever possible, use buzz-words relevant to the job you are seeking.

- Your resume should be one page. Since some employers scan resumes looking for key phrases, make certain that you do your research and include phrases appropriate to the type of work you are seeking.

- Do not use personal pronouns.

- Do not use abbreviations. The only exceptions are state abbreviations and USA.

- Do not use periods in abbreviations. (Incorrect: U.S.A., Correct: USA)

- Write out all numbers up to and including nine. Use numerals for 10 to 999,999 (except at the beginning of a sentence).

The samples on the following pages are examples of resumes that focus on accomplishments and can therefore be customized to specific jobs or organizations. It is the preferred format, but additional samples are provided in subsequent pages as well.

# First Name and Last Name
Address Telephone  Email Address

**EDUCATION**
College of University, City, SC
**Bachelors Degree, Month and Year you graduated (will graduate)**
Major:
GPA: If over 3.0

**EXPERIENCE**
INSERT COMPANY'S NAME (ALL CAPS not bolded),                          City, State and Country
Title of the position (bold)                                                                     Month year – Month year
- Insert your accomplishment statements (2 to 4). Keep to 1 line (concise, clear, direct).
- Begin each statement with a strong action verb and end each statement with a period.
- Each should highlight an achievement and/or value-adding experience, quantified.
- Accomplishment statements should be relevant to the job you are targeting.

INSERT COMPANY'S NAME (ALL CAPS not bolded),                          City, State and Country
Title of the position (bold)                                                                     Month year – Month year
- Insert your accomplishment statements (2 to 4). Keep to 1 line (concise, clear, direct).
- Begin each statement with a strong action verb and end each statement with a period.
- Each should highlight an achievement and/or value-adding experience, quantified.

INSERT COMPANY'S NAME (ALL CAPS not bolded),                          City, State and Country
Title of the position (bold)                                                                     Month year – Month year
- Insert your accomplishment statements (2 to 4). Keep to 1 line (concise, clear, direct).
- Begin each statement with a strong action verb and end each statement with a period.
- Each should highlight an achievement and/or value-adding experience, quantified.

**LEADERSHIP ACTIVITIES**
- Insert any leadership positions you have held on or off campus if relevant (clubs, teams, church, etc.).

**COMMUNITY ACTIVITIES**
- Insert any community service projects, volunteer work, etc. here.

**TECHNICAL SKILLS**
- If you have unique technical skills, insert them here. Microsoft and internet proficiency is assumed. Only list unique programs or systems you are proficient in.

**HONORS & AWARDS**
- Insert your non-academic and academic awards and honors.

# JOHN SMITH
1234 Main Street, Columbia, SC 29201 • (803) 121-1212
@email.sc.edu • LinkedIn link

## EDUCATION

**Darla Moore School of Business, University of South Carolina**                Columbia, SC
*Bachelor of Science, Business Administration*                                   May 2020
**Major**: Finance
**Minor**: Spanish
**GPA**: 3.5
**Award**: Dean's List

**Darla Moore School of Business Study Abroad**                   Buenos Aires, Argentina
Language and Culture Classes                                                    May 2018

## PROFESSIONAL EXPERIENCE

**Clothing Store**                                                              Columbia, SC
*Sales Associate*                                                    January 2018-Present
- Exceeded corporate sales goals by 5% by providing exceptional service and initiating client conversations to determine personal preferences.

**XYZ Restaurant**                                                             Baltimore, MD
*Waitress/Server*                                                               Summer 2017
- Managed $1,000-$3,000 cash transactions daily utilizing attention to detail.
- Trained three new servers in daily operations ensuring efficiency and excellent customer service.

## LEADERSHIP

**Student Success Center**                                                      Columbia, SC
*Peer Tutor*                                                         August 2017-Present
- Provide peer tutoring to three students a week and help develop tools and study habits to increase overall GPA.
- Differentiate lessons for individual learning styles, resulting in 100% passing rate.

**ABC High School**                                                            Atlanta, GA
*Class President*                                                September 2015-May 2016
- Led Executive Board meetings and helped make decisions regarding policies, school events and fundraisers, to improve the school experience for 3500 students.

## ACTIVITIES/INVOLVEMENT

**Alpha Kappa Psi**                                                            Columbia, SC
*Member*                                                             August 2017-Present
- Participate in professionalism events and assist with recruiting two new members.

## LANGUAGES        SPANISH: proficient    ENGLISH: native

# FIRSTNAME LASTNAME

+1 (555) 444-4444 | name@email.sc.edu | www.LinkedIn.com/in/FirstnameLastname

## EDUCATION

| | | |
|---|---|---|
| University of South Carolina | Darla Moore School of Business | Columbia, SC USA | May 2020 |

**Double Major:** Marketing and Management — GPA: 3.56
**Minor**: French

Institute for American Universities | The Aix Center Aix-en-Provence, France — January–May 2019
**Studied:** Intercultural Management, Globalization, Professional French, Art — GPA: 3.76

## HONORS/AWARDS

USC's Outstanding Woman of the Year finalist, Emerging Leader, Who's Who of USC Students, Marketing Scholar

## INTERNSHIP EXPERIENCE

**Communications and Brands Intern** | ABC Firm — Greenville, SC USA — June – August 2018
- Conducted in-depth research and produced plan to leverage social media for recruiting.
- Strategized to provide necessary items for 3K+ press members for the 2012 Detroit Auto Show.
- Facilitated the distribution of 6K email-based surveys for the Career Management team; addressed concerns and questions in a timely manner.

## PROFESSIONAL EXPERIENCE

**Marketing Agent** | ABC Supermarket — Columbia, SC USA — August 2018 – Present
- Lead team of 10 Marketing Scholars in designing plan to build brand equity and generate exposure within targeted niche market for nationwide organic supermarket.
- Conducted extensive research on target markets and managed peers throughout brainstorming and plan development to facilitate an effective marketing plan.

**Consultant** | ABC Company, INC. — Columbia, SC USA — August – December 2017
- Co-led student team in creating a comprehensive export plan and international market entry strategy for a Spartanburg, SC company.
- Analyzed and researched Greenfield multi-national business opportunities and distilled complex data into actionable solutions in accordance with client needs and opportunities.
- Designed complete marketing strategy to yield results in new industries in the UAE and Mexico as well as in the US domestic markets which included strategies for buying and procurement with the government.

**Resident Mentor** | USC University Housing — Columbia, SC USA — August 2016 – May 2017
- Managed and supervised a university residence hall floor of 36 ethnically-diverse first-year students.
- Worked cohesively on building a staff of 30 fellow Resident Mentors.
- Enforced University rules to result in a safe and orderly environment; developed mediation and conflict resolution skills.

**Team Leader** | Principles of Management Class — Columbia, SC USA — January – May 2017
- Led a team of 25 peers in the research, crafting, and presentation of a cohesive business plan to a local start-up.
- Designed plans for finance/investment, operations, full-scale marketing as well as community and social media strategies resulting in continued success in the community.

## LEADERSHIP EXPERIENCE

**Vice President of Professional Development** | Alpha Kappa Psi, Professional Business Fraternity — August 2018 – Present
- Envisioned, planned, and implemented 10 events that developed personal and professional success for 125 members, the chapter, and the University.
- Pioneered and directed first ever student-led consulting team to provide philanthropic solutions to local programs and firms in the community.

**International Business Advisory Council Representative** | Darla Moore School of Business — August – December 2017
- Elected to work with peers to improve the function of the nation's top International Business Program.

**Secretary of Student Services** | Executive Cabinet of USC Student Body President — August 2016 – May 2017
- Led successful efforts to advocate the inclusion of off-campus dining services in conjunction with current Carolina Card offerings.

**LANGUAGE**    FRENCH    Oral | Advanced    Reading | Intermediate    Writing | Intermediate

**IT SKILLS**    Adobe Photoshop, Illustrator, Bridge, InDesign, Paramount Acceptance

**ACTIVITIES**    American Marketing Association, Carolina Finance and Investment Association, Buddies Beyond Borders, USC Dance Marathon (2017), French Club

**INTERESTS**    Inbound Marketing, Graphic Design

# JOHN N. DOE

1313 Cocky Street, Anywhere, SC 12345 • Cell Phone (444) 555-5555
jdoe@email.sc.edu • www.linkedin.com/in/johnndoe

## EDUCATION

University of South Carolina                                                    Columbia, SC
Bachelor of Science: Finance, Darla Moore School of Business                    May 2018
Minor: Spanish
Cumulative GPA: 3.5/4.0

Darla Moore School of Business Study Abroad                         Monterrey, Nuevo Leon, MEXICO
*Instituto Technologico de Estudios Superiores*                                 May 2017

## PROFESSIONAL EXPERIENCE

**Cocky Mortgage Corporation**                                                  Columbia, SC
*Search Advertising Intern*                                            August 2016 – Present
- Analyze digital data pertaining to search queries and keywords by identifying patterns and monitoring performance to increase search results by 15%.
- Review online advertising campaigns to maximize and increase web traffic and lead-ins.
- Create ad copy and keyword research that has generated a 10% increase in company conversion rates.
- Provide evaluation reports to management that increase financial statement accuracy for accounts worth over $15 million.

**Cocky Bank**                                                                  Charlotte, NC
*Commercial Banking Intern*                                          May 2016 – August 2016
- Developed financial models to structure and optimize transactions with commercial clients.
- Conducted analyses on client capital structure and prepared presentations for financing proposals and new business development.
- Assisted managers with portfolio management, business development and financial analysis for the upcoming fiscal year.

## LEADERSHIP EXPERIENCE

**Anglers at USC, University of South Carolina**                                Columbia, SC
*Treasurer*                                                            August 2016 – Present
- Oversee an $8,000 budget while monitoring programming, social, and meeting expenditures.
- Coordinate fundraising strategies that successfully raised $2,500 for club activities in 2015.

**Alpha Kappa Psi, Beta Upsilon Chapter**                                       Columbia, SC
*Vice President of Membership*                                       January 2016 – May 2016
- Organized recruitment and selection activities that resulted in a 20% increase in pledge class enrollment from the previous year.
- Coordinated bi-weekly pledge class events for 35 participants that included leading weekly meetings, organizing pledge class events, and conducting formal ceremonies.

## RELEVANT SKILLS AND ACTIVITIES

- Habitat for Humanity, Boys & Girls Club, USC Dance Marathon
- Proficiency in Microsoft Office, Dreamweaver, Java, and HTML
- Languages: Spanish (proficient), Chinese (intermediate)

**JOHN SMITH**
123 Main Street, Columbia, SC 29229
+1 (803) 123-4567
JohnSmith@email.sc.edu

EDUCATION

MOORE SCHOOL OF BUSINESS, University of South Carolina                    Columbia, SC USA
**Bachelor of Science, Business Administration**                                          May 2018
**Majors:** Operations and Supply Chain, Management
**GPA**: 3.5
**Honors:** Dean's List, Life Scholarship

EXPERIENCE

UNITED STATES ARMY                                                     Ansbach, GERMANY
**Aircraft Mechanic and Service Technician**                        September 2008 – May 2013
Led soldiers in personal development as well as professional growth within the ranks of enlisted servicemen.
Served as a turbine engine mechanic troubleshooting complex systems and performing scheduled maintenance.
- Deployed to Iraq where unit received meritorious unit commendation for excellent performance.
- Coordinated and completed training of 150 new recruits while deployed to Iraq.
- Mentored 50 Junior Enlisted to improve military bearing and set personal goals.
- Maintained over $300,000 worth of calibrated equipment, providing 100% mission readiness.
- Performed scheduled/ unscheduled maintenance and troubleshot turbine engines on Army aircraft.
- Awarded *Army Achievement Medal* for exceptional support of several aircraft.
- Provided over 1,800 hours of aircraft maintenance while deployed resulting in being awarded the *Army Commendation Medal*.

PANERA                                                                    Rochester, NY USA
**Team Member and Shift Manager**                                      March 2006 – May 2008
Opened and closed the store operations. Handled customer issues as well as general worker relations.
- Monitored and reinforced safety procedures keeping store in compliance with high food standards.
- Trained and maintained schedules of 15 workers, ensuring proper coverage per shift.
- Served approximately 100 guests per shift, upselling items to increase sales.
- Provided excellent customer service, encouraging repeat business and awarded *Employee of the Month*.

LEADERSHIP

ALPHA KAPPA PSI, business fraternity                                   Columbia, SC USA
**Treasurer**                                                          August 2016- present
Collect dues and manage finance for organization of 150 members, with a budget of $15,000.
- Organize finance books and budget for four annual events using Microsoft Excel, staying within budget.
- Network with professionals and help plan events to increase members' knowledge of industry.

VOLUNTEERISM

BOYS AND GIRLS CLUB OF AMERICA                                         Columbia, SC USA
**Volunteer**                                                          August 2016 –present
Mentor young students to increase grades and self-confidence, while maintaining friendship and guidance.

| | | |
|---|---|---|
| LANGUAGES | GERMAN: Intermediate | ENGLISH: Native |
| IT SKILLS | Microsoft Office, Java, C++, Social Media | |
| ACTIVITIES | Freshman Dorm Council, Intramural Sports on campus | |
| CERTIFICATIONS | CPR Red Cross Certified, Boating License | |

## PORTFOLIO—YES OR NO?

Should you develop a digital and physical portfolio? Absolutely! Having both a physical and digital portfolio can be a great benefit, especially if your search targets are varied. To be competitive in today's marketplace, it is becoming more and more essential to represent your work and talents in this way.

A digital portfolio can complement a physical portfolio. Both are developed after your resume is completed and they are another way to confirm your strengths and values. They do not include or replace your resume. They provide employers additional information about you and your work, and it is becoming more and more common for employers to make final hiring decisions based on these portfolios.

The physical portfolio is a great "leave behind" after an interview and may help keep you "top of mind" after you leave. They can provide you with that needed edge showing how much you want the job.

If you decide to create either a physical or digital portfolio, consider the following:

- Use a graphic designer and print shop, and remember to listen to their recommendations.

- Be concise. Show 15-20 pieces that will prove you are qualified for the job.

- Study the company's website to learn about the company and what strengths/values they are expecting in candidates.

- Tailor the portfolio to the job and the company's needs.

- Have a portfolio that can be easily edited for other companies and jobs.

- Place the best and most relevant work first and finish with strong pieces that reflect your strengths and values.

- Include a variety of examples of work you have done. These can be from school, internships, part-time jobs, hobbies, and community activities.

- You can use a sequence of photos, spreadsheets, graphs, and anything else that shows your thought process, development of ideas, analytical thinking, creativity, and innovation.

- Know your portfolio and how to use it in an interview to sell yourself.

# BE INTENTIONAL

- USE YOUR RESUME AS A SALES AID.
- PLAN A GREAT PRESENTATION ON YOURSELF.
- BE SINCERE AND BELIEVABLE.
- FIGURE OUT WHAT MOTIVATES YOU BESIDES MONEY, AND BE READY TO TALK ABOUT IT.

# CHAPTER 7
# Preparing for a Successful Interview

OUTCOMES:

**I WILL UNDERSTAND WHAT WILL BE EXPECTED OF ME IN THE INTERVIEW PROCESS.**

**I WILL GAIN CONFIDENCE IN MYSELF BECAUSE I RECOGNIZE MY ABILITY TO PROVE MY STRENGTHS AND SKILLS.**

**I WILL LEARN HOW TO MAKE THE INTERVIEWER'S JOB EASIER.**

## BIRKMAN AND THE INTERVIEW PROCESS

Being interviewed by strangers who hold your fate in their hands is typically an unpleasant and unnerving experience. Some of us are naturally more comfortable in this arena, while others would rather face just about anything other than that first handshake and the all-important prompt to "Tell me about yourself."

Understanding your natural talents in this area is crucial as you continue the preparation process, anticipating your upcoming interviews. With that in mind, we will again look to your Birkman results to learn more about the best ways you can prepare for this inevitable part of the job search process.

Let's start by looking at the ways in which you are at your best in an interview.

**Please locate and read, "How You Approach Interviews, Section A: When you are at your best in the interview."**

### EXERCISE 1

Do you agree with most of the statements in this report? Yes/No

Did you answer "no"? If so, your next step is to show this list to someone in your life who is close to you and ask them if they agree or disagree with these statements. If they agree with these statements and you do not, it is likely that you are currently viewing yourself in a negative light, probably due to the current state of your employment.

Take this as an opportunity to celebrate your natural strengths in this area, even if you feel quite removed from them at the moment. As your confidence returns, you will likely embrace these characteristics and use them to your advantage. It will be important that you experience an attitude shift in this area prior to an actual interview if these strengths are to be leveraged. This is something only you can accomplish, and it may require a great deal of intentionality. Once you are feeling more intune with these strengths please proceed to the next section and complete the associated exercises.

### EXERCISE 2

1. Think back through previous interviews and recall a time when these characteristics clearly played to your advantage. Record that memory in the space provided below.

2. Has there been a time in your past when you performed badly in an interview and these strengths did not play to your advantage? If so, record that memory in the space provided below.

3. If you answered "yes" to previous question, please spend a few minutes contemplating what influences contributed to your lack of success in that situation and record your thoughts in the space provided below.

Various factors contribute to unsuccessful interviews. For now, however, we will focus on the factors that tie directly to the Birkman and the "needs" we have been discussing since Chapter 1.

**Please refer back to the "How You Approach Job Interviews" report and this time refer to "Section B: When you are less at ease in an interview."**

Now, look back at your answer to #3 in Exercise 2. Do any of these Birkman statements coincide with your thoughts as to why you were unsuccessful in a previous interview? In other words, did these behaviors manifest in previous situations?

These are real risks for you in an interview setting. These are, as you probably assumed, the stress behaviors that may rear their ugly head when you are in the pressure cooker that can be an interview.

Birkman provides a few suggestions for how to prepare for, and hopefully avoid, these potential stress reactions. **Please refer back to the "How You Approach Job Interviews" report and this time refer to "Section C: Preparing for the interview."**

The only aspect of an interview you can actually control is your preparation and reactions. You cannot control the interviewer, which is why it is crucial that you be aware of your tendencies and work hard to control them and prepare for situations that could potentially trigger them.

## UNDERSTANDING THE LAY OF THE LAND

Understanding yourself and the ways in which you might respond in the process is only a part of understanding the interview itself. You also must understand the other player(s) in the process, the interviewer(s).

### THE VARIOUS ROLES OF THE PLAYERS – YOU AND THEM

Good or bad, most interviewers make up their minds about the applicant in the first five minutes. The rest of the time is spent confirming their opinion, whether it is positive or negative. As they do this through questioning, which will be discussed a little later, they will also be gathering necessary information to fill out forms that are required by their company. These forms contain the questions they are to ask, along with a place for them to record your answers. Also, there will most likely be an Applicant Evaluation Form for the Personal Interview. This form is where the interviewer(s) record their reactions and opinions of you. These forms are required by Human Resources to assure that all applicants are treated the same.

With this in mind, please understand your actual role in the process, as well as that of the interviewer(s).

**YOUR ROLE IS TO BUILD CREDIBILITY WITH THE INTERVIEWER, SELL YOURSELF, MAKE THE JOB OF DECISION MAKING EASIER FOR THE INTERVIEWER, AND GET A PROMISE FOR THE SECOND INTERVIEW.**

In most situations, the first interviewer does not make the final decision. They will re-interview or turn you down, or refer to another manager. In some very rare cases, they can make an offer. Regardless, you must get a commitment for another interview or negotiate time to consider an offer if it is made.

Please remember the person sitting in front of you has the power or influence to hire and wants to know the following things about you:

- Why are you interviewing with this potential employer?
- What can you do for them? (your strengths and skills for their needs and goals)
- What kind of person are you? (character, strengths, skills, and special knowledge)
- What distinguishes you from other people/applicants?
- Can they afford you?

You, as the applicant need to ask the same questions in a different form:

- What does the job involve?
- How do my strengths, skills, and motivational factors match the job?
- Does this corporate culture, and the people who work here, meet my needs as discussed earlier in this book?
- What can I do to convince them of my strengths and uniqueness, differentiating me from others?
- What can I do to convince them to hire me at the salary I need or want?

In addition, the role of the interviewer is to gather the necessary information to make a documented recommendation to their boss and/or human resources. They may require two or three interviews – make their job easier by keeping in mind the paperwork that will be required of them. An example of an evaluation form will require they fill out the following information:

- source of referral
- position applied for
- strengths with regard to meeting job needs (they will refer to written Principal Qualifications and Duties/ Job Descriptions)
- shortcomings with regard to meeting job needs (make sure any weaknesses that you describe in the interview are not important to the job needs)
- overall evaluation of applicant (summary of strengths and shortcomings as they affect their decision)
- an explanation of disposition of applicant.

KEEPING ALL OF THIS IN MIND, YOU MUST BE PREPARED, IN ADVANCE, TO SHARE THE **TOP 3-4** THINGS YOU BELIEVE THIS INTERVIEWER/EMPLOYER SHOULD KNOW ABOUT YOU.

This should be based on a clear understanding of your strengths and accomplishments as discussed in the previous chapters. You should be able to elaborate on all of your strengths and accomplishments, so you must be strategic and select those that are most relevant to this particular situation.

Before each interview you should spend significant time researching the company and studying the job description (read more about this in Chapter 13) in order to determine the most important things you want them to know about you. This means, of course, that you must be fully versed in your own strengths and accomplishments and prepared to talk about them in meaningful ways.

## WHAT IS A BEHAVIORAL INTERVIEW?

Many interviewers will use what is known as a Behavioral Interview. This type of interview is based on the premise that past behavior is the best predictor of future performance. The following are true of this type of interview.

- Questions are developed around the traits and skills they deem necessary for succeeding in the position, organization, or field.
- These questions require you to give evidence of your skills, experience, and personal qualities, not just list them.
- You must develop a list of experiences that cover the skills and characteristics required for the position. Your work on defining your accomplishments earlier in the book will be the foundation for preparing for these types of interviews. Have your notes from Chapter 5 close by.

The following are some examples of often-used behavioral-based interviewing prompts and questions:

- Describe a situation where you had to accomplish an independent project.
- Tell me about a time that you were a member of a team. What was your role? What did the team accomplish?
- Describe a business situation which created stress for you.
- Give me an example of a situation where you had conflict with another employee in a work situation. How did you handle it?
- Give me an example of a project you completed successfully.
- What is your leadership style? Give me an example of a situation where you exhibited leadership.
- Give me an example of a situation where you made an improvement in your prior business situation.
- Tell me about a goal you set and how you achieved it.
- Give me an example of a situation where you had to work under pressure.
- Describe a situation where you managed people to accomplish a task.

In order to prepare for this type of interview you must be very prepared to talk about what you have accomplished in the past. The best way to do this is to follow what is known in the human resources field as the STAR method. In a nutshell, this technique is designed to see if you are a good fit for their job. Your job is to prove that you are by highlighting your past successes in a succinct and relevant way. Here is how it works.

**SITUATION**
YOUR JOB: Explain, briefly, the background and the situation you found yourself in.

**TASK**
YOUR JOB: Explain, specifically, what you had to accomplish, overcome, or solve.

**ACTIONS**
YOUR JOB: Explain, specifically, what you did and why you did what you did to accomplish what you accomplished.

**RESULTS**
YOUR JOB: Quantify and/or qualify the results of your actions. Did you solve it? Did it save or make money? Did it improve a process, a relationship, etc.? How did you **add value**?

## EXERCISE 3

With the STAR method in mind, look back at Chapter 5 and note the strength/competency you listed as your top strength. Use the following template to craft a story explaining the accomplishment you selected, transforming the explanation into a STAR interview answer.

## S – SITUATION:

Briefly describe the situation and setting for your listener.

## T – TASK:

Explain, specifically, what you had to accomplish, overcome, or solve.

## A – ACTIONS:

Explain, specifically, what you did and why you did what you did.

## R – RESULTS:

Quantify and/or qualify the results of your actions. Did you solve it? Did it save or make money? Did it improve a process, a relationship, etc.? How did you ADD VALUE?

## SKILL/STRENGTHS:

Finally, list what skills and strengths you utilized in this situation.

## NOW FOR THE HEAVY LIFTING

Although you did much of the heavy lifting in Chapter 5 as you thought through your accomplishments, in order for that work to actually help you in the interview, you must do the following:

### EXERCISE 4

Use the STAR template on the previous page to craft STAR statements for each of the remaining four strengths/competencies you listed in your top five in Chapter 5. This will be tedious and time consuming, but if this work is done well, the interview will go well. This may be the most important exercise in this book, so please take it seriously.

**S**

**T**

**A**

**R**

## INTERVIEW DOS AND DON'TS

Regardless of interview type or the experience level of the person conducting the interview, there are some universal "truths" you need to know. Below are some of the obvious Do's and Don'ts:

### DO'S

1. Wear business attire for all interviews, which means: wear a suit! This means that the jacket and the pants match. For men, a tie, shoes, and a belt should match. Ladies, pantsuits are usually fine, and if you do wear a skirt make sure it is at least knee-length.

2. Maintain eye contact.

3. Assure that you have a firm handshake – you want to achieve impact from your appearance and confidence.

4. Listen to the questions and take time to make sure you understand the question before formulating your response.

5. Be clear and concise when you ask your planned questions – jot down the answers and make notes during the interview. This shows interest in the other person and gives you time to pause and think.

### DON'TS:

1. It is NEVER appropriate to take a call, read a text, or check social media in an interview. NEVER! Leave your cell phone in the car.

2. Don't let the interviewer control the entire interview by taking all of the time with their questions. Remember that you should be prepared with 3-4 things you need them to know about you. Make sure you share that information.

3. Don't interrupt them, but make sure you have enough control to achieve what you need to accomplish.

## QUESTIONS TO CONSIDER BEFORE THE INTERVIEW

The following questions are ones you are likely to encounter, thus you should prepare for them beforehand in order to be successful in your answers.

### 1. Tell me about yourself.

- Some interviewers ask this to simply break the ice. Others ask to see what you view as important. And, others ask it to see if you will share something they can't legally ask.
- Your job is to prepare a 1-2 minute "elevator speech" for use when answering this question. This should focus on your strengths and skills and include basic information about the 3-4 things you want them to know about you. This is your chance to set the stage. You should not include personal information in this response.

### 2. Why are you here? Why do you want to work with us?

- This gives you the opportunity to demonstrate what you have learned about the company and your initiative in developing your individual marketing plan. We will talk more about company research later in Chapter 14.

### 3. What distinguishes you from other applicants?

- Relate your strengths, skills, and motivating factors to the assumed needs and goals of the company. This relates back to the work you did in chapters 4 and 5. You must be completely aware of and comfortable discussing your strengths and accomplishments.

### 4. What kind of salary/income are you expecting?

- Answer with a question, i.e., "What is the salary range for this position?" If there is no range or they are not saying, respond with: "I think a position like this would be in the range of $ ." Have a specific amount that you want to start at with the opportunity to increase with a Pay for Performance increase in the near future.

### 5. What do you want or expect in a job?

- Opportunity to perform – be rewarded – be recognized – and advance in responsibilities only after establishing a positive track record.

### 6. How long would it take for you to be a top performer?

- "Could you give me a time that it has taken in the past for others, and I will beat that time by 3 to 6 months." If they don't give you a time for the average or top performers – be realistic and say six months to one year.

### 7. Are you willing to relocate?

- "Yes. I would have preferences, but I would not let those get in the way of this job and opportunity." Get the job offer first and then decide if you want to relocate.

## 8. Where would you like to be in five years?

- You need to seriously think about where you truly want to be in 5 years. You need to be specific enough to show you have thought about this, but general enough to ensure you don't talk yourself out of the job.
- You could ask a question like this if you want to learn more before answering: "What is the usual next step in advancement – job position – and in what length of time on average?"

## 9. How long would you stay with us?

- "As long as we both feel that I am making significant contributions to the company."

## 10. What is a typical day like with your present job? If you are not currently employed, describe a previous job or your current role as a student.

- "I'm responsible for ... and held accountable for ... ."
- Keep your answer brief, but emphasize strengths, skills, tasks, and motivating factors.

## 11. Why are you leaving your present job?

- • Don't be negative and don't change answers. If you were laid off, you need to briefly explain the circumstances and then move on.
- "I believe your company will offer more of a challenge and opportunities for personal development or growth."

## 12. What would an ideal working environment look like for you?

- "Having a manager or boss who would: ... ." How you complete this sentence should be directly related to what you now know you need based on your Birkman results. BUT, always keep in mind that no boss will ever meet all of your needs.

## 13. How would you describe your present company? Boss?

- Be positive. Never, NEVER say anything negative about anyone or an organization.
- You could always answer with something simple like this: "They provided me with experience and opportunities to prove myself."

## 14. Have you made suggestions or ideas that were implemented by your present manager or company?

- If they ask this, it is the perfect opening to share an accomplishment using the STAR method. This is why you decide before the interview the 3-4 things you want them to know about you.
- Be brief, but describe in detail and share results. Refer back to your STAR stories.

## 15. With your present company or last position, what were three or four of your significant accomplishments?

- You should be completely ready for this question if you did the STAR statements for all of your accomplishments. Answer completely, touching on every aspect of the STAR technique.

## 16. Why haven't you found a new position before now?

- If still working, emphasize time requirements of present job and limited time for search and interviewing. If you are a student, simply share your year, major, and anticipated graduation date.
- If not presently working, share that you have been working hard to complete a full self-assessment process to ensure you find a job that is the right fit. This is in their best interest too!

## 17. When we do a reference check, what will they say are your greatest strengths and weaknesses?

- Keep in mind that reference checks should be referred to Human Resources and they will only confirm dates of employment.
- Answer with your strengths in different words but the same meaning.
- With weaknesses – only give ones that are not needed for the job or can be turned into attributes or positives.

## 18. Can you work under pressures, time goals, deadlines, etc.?

- Be completely comfortable with your Birkman strengths and share this here.

## 19. In your present position or recent past experiences, what problems did you identify and solve?

- This is another opportunity to use your STAR stories.

## 20. What other companies or type of jobs are you considering or interviewing for?

- Keep your answer related only to this company's field.
- Be honest if you are currently interviewing with other competitive companies, but you do not have to say which ones. DO say, however, if you have been invited in for other interviews and they have shown interest in you, but that you would prefer the job and company you are presently interviewing for. Be able to answer the question: "Why would you prefer us?"

## DIGITAL/ELECTRONIC INTERVIEWING METHODS

Not long ago digital and electronic interviewing techniques were the exception, but in today's world it is very likely that your first encounter with an employer will be through your webcam. Why? Because the technology is available and it saves employers time and money. Even more so than telephone interviewing, this will require intentional preparation.

- The "pre-interview" prep is similar to a face to face interview
- Be ready with the STAR Stories
- Do the Employer research
- Be ready to sell yourself as a solution

You might be recorded using prompts so a recruiter can watch later, or there might be a recruiter live on screen. Either way, remember that they are likely using some type of artificial intelligence to assess the video.

Record yourself and listen/watch for the following:

- Are your STAR stories clear?
- Are you rambling?
- Are you doing something annoying like clicking a pen or biting a lip.
- Make sure the background isn't cluttered or inappropriate
- Don't have pets in the room
- Ensure the environment is quiet
- Dress professionally
- Sit up straight
- Smile
- Be authentic

Finally, please remember that the Telephone Screening Interview is still very common, and all of the same rules apply. Be prepared and treat it just like a face to face interview or digital experience. Do your homework on the employer, be prepared with your STAR stories and ensure the environment is quiet and interruptions will be minimal.

Remember, the digital and telephone interviewing experiences are the first step towards an actual face to face encounter with the employer. Don't take these experiences lightly!

## INTERVIEW BLUNDERS

In most any interview you are likely to blunder a question or two. That said, there are ways to recover and regain the interest of the recruiter. Here are a couple of pointers to remember if you feel the interview is not going well.

1. If you believe the interviewer has lost interest or is bored, stop talking and ask a question. This will usually inject energy into the conversation and allow the interviewer to become re-engaged in the process.

2. There will be times when you are asked a question for which you genuinely don't have an answer. This could be a behavioral question and you have not had an experience like the one referenced, or it could be a question that simply stumps you. Use the following as a guideline for tackling these tough situations:

    a. BEHAVIORAL QUESTION: If you have truly not had an experience related to the question, share that you have not had such an experience and talk about what you would do if you were to encounter such a situation in the future.

b. STUMPED: Ask the interviewer to repeat the question, and if you still don't know how to answer, be honest and tell the interviewer that you don't know. Making something up at this point will cause more harm than good, so being honest is your best bet.

3. If you get off track and realize that you are not making sense, stop and ask if you can start over.

## FINAL THOUGHTS ON INTERVIEWING

The more time and effort you put into the exercises outlined in this chapter, and the entire book, the better prepared you will be for other questions and the interview. If, up until now, you have skimmed the sections of this book that required you to think, work, or write, now is a good time to go back and actually complete the exercises. You won't be sorry!

# BE INTENTIONAL

- BE POSITIVE.
- DRESS APPROPRIATELY, ALWAYS.
- AVOID PESSIMISM AND SARCASM.
- SMILE AND LEAN FORWARD; BOTH SHOW INTEREST.
- PRACTICE INTERVIEWING ANY TIME YOU ARE OFFERED THE CHANCE, EITHER AT SCHOOL OR ELSEWHERE.

## CHAPTER 8

# Networking

The term networking at times has a negative connotation, conjuring up images of a used car salesman or that slick, slippery guy at a cocktail party. While there are folks who take the concept to the extreme, put aside your preconceived notions and consider the value of networking in securing the right opportunity for your future. Let's discuss why networking is so important before we look to your Birkman results for some insight into how easy it may, or may not be, for you.

## BECOMING A REFERRAL

Dictionary.com provides this definition of **refer**: "to direct the attention or thoughts of." It also states that a **referral** is "a person recommended to someone or for something." Thus, becoming a referral means that someone else has directed an employer's attention towards you, and they have recommended you for a job. Put that way, it should be clear why this would be a desired outcome in your search. Clearly, the best way to create a competitive advantage on your job search is to be a referral.

Hiring for any position is expensive, particularly if the wrong person is hired. For this reason, companies pay thousands of dollars to obtain job candidates from employment agencies, internet and print ads, college recruiting, and job fairs. Because of the expense of these approaches, employers are turning more and more to referrals, because they are free. They simply need someone they trust to recommend a qualified candidate.

This becomes even more important for you as the job seeker when you consider that many open jobs do not make it to the open job market because they are filled by referrals. It is estimated that 60 to 70 percent of open jobs in the private sector are filled by referrals. Now do you see why you want to be one of those referrals?

So, how does this work? First and foremost, referrals are usually made by employees of companies, although they can also come from other sources like professors or customers.

FOR THIS REASON, IT IS CRUCIAL THAT YOU COMMUNICATE TO AS MANY PEOPLE AS POSSIBLE THAT YOU ARE IN THE JOB MARKET. IT IS ESPECIALLY IMPORTANT THAT ANYONE YOU KNOW WORKING FOR A COMPANY YOU ARE TARGETING IS AWARE OF YOUR SITUATION.

Employees are most likely to refer people who they feel will be good performers and have a good background for their company. They generally will not refer poor performers, because that would reflect poorly on them. In addition, they will usually share information about the company and the interviewing process with the candidate which can be a huge benefit during the interview process.

## CASE STUDY EXAMPLES

Let's look at a few real life cases to emphasize why networking and referrals are so important.

### ACTUAL CASE 1: COLLEGE GRADUATE NETWORKING

A recent college graduate is seeking a job in accounting. She decides that she wants to try to become a referral. She is going to use the networking approach. First she checks with all her relatives (who work for a variety of companies). She asks for possible contacts and gives them copies of her resume. She then contacts students in her class and her professors and gives them copies of her resume and seeks company contacts from them. She contacts graduates of her school who are already out working. She also goes to her college Career Management Center, repeating the same process. Overall she has made at least 100 job-related contacts. Eventually, 2 job openings arise from this process. She receives information from the employees who referred her about the interviewing process. She interviews for both jobs and receives an offer for one of the jobs.

It is said that the average person knows at least 250 people. If you contact 100 people, you can potentially reach 25,000; if you contact 200, you can potentially reach 50,000. Consequently, networking is clearly the best method for reaching as many people as possible, and becoming a referral as often as possible. If you are a referral, you will have some inside knowledge about the company. An employee who can vouch for your character and potential performance will be recommending you, which means you have jumped over other candidates who are applying through traditional processes. The company will be saving money in its recruiting process and knows that the candidate comes from an employee or a trusted outside source (professor, career counselor, or customer).

## ACTUAL CASE 2: MANAGEMENT REFERRAL

A management employee of a major company has begun a job search. He contacts his friends and business associates to begin the networking process. A friend who is an employee of another major company refers him to an open job in his company. This company has a reputation for having a very difficult selection process for management candidates. The candidate gets a briefing on the interview process. The company uses a behavioral, targeted selection process (STAR method) with a series of group interviews that cover problem solving, style of management, teamwork, and technical issues. The candidate prepares for the interview process by rehearsing behavioral questions covering all of the issues. He completes the interviewing process successfully and is offered the job. Without the briefing from the friend who referred him, this interview could have been a disaster.

There are additional reasons why an employee of a company would want to refer qualified individuals to their company. Many companies are so interested in referrals that they create incentive or bonus programs to have their employees generate more referrals. They will pay cash ($500 to $1000) for each referral, or give company products or credits to buy company products. One consumer electronics company gives credits that can be used to purchase their products from inventory.

The key is that the same candidate could cost 25 percent of the salary if an employment agency places the candidate ($10,000 fee for a $40,000 job placement), or $3,000 to $6,000 for a decent print ad in major market publications or large ads in online job boards. Consequently, the best way for a company to get candidates is through referrals, and the best way for a candidate to get to a company is by being a referral.

## ACTUAL CASE 3: THE LAST CANDIDATE FOR A SENIOR JOB

A major company was conducting a search for a Vice President of Operations. The search firm had presented 13 candidates, but the company was not completely satisfied with the candidates. During the same period that the search was being conducted, a vice president (VP) from another company in a similar business was given notice because her company was being sold. The VP who was given notice networked with all her resources. She had wide business connections. One of the people she networked with was a boss who knew the search firm that was handling the open job. The former boss referred her to the search firm. They interviewed her and presented her as a candidate for the open VP job.

The boss and the search firm prepped her on the interview process, and she did a comprehensive study of the company and all its businesses. Needless to say she got the job. She was the 14th and last candidate. Networking paid off for her.

## HOW TO NETWORK EFFECTIVELY

Effective networking is always going to involve a conversation with another human being, so do not be fooled into thinking that you can do all of this online.

> THAT BEING SAID, SOCIAL MEDIA NETWORKS NOW PLAY A MAJOR ROLE IN THE NETWORKING PROCESS. THEIR PURPOSE IS TO MAKE CONTACT WITH LARGE NUMBERS OF PEOPLE AT ONCE, BUT THE END RESULT SHOULD ALWAYS BE A CONVERSATION, IF AT ALL POSSIBLE.

Your online contacts from Instagram, Twitter, and LinkedIn, or anywhere else, could be the ones supporting your application to a new job, or the ones to let you know about a new opportunity in the first place. Having a strong network of supporters is incredibly valuable in any career, and even more so when looking for the next/best opportunity.

Managing your online network has one additional important caveat: you are not "collecting friends." Many people get lost in the numbers game, but you have to ask yourself this question: what is the value of adding one additional name to your contacts list if they never see/hear a thing from you? It should be clear that being a silent member of your own network is not going to get you results, and that having the most number of connections is fairly meaningless compared to having a few people that are engaged with and supportive of you.

With networking, connections should be leads to future conversations. The same is true in social media, but the barriers associated with these conversations are much smaller. You should join conversations, particularly on LinkedIn, to demonstrate your interests and expertise. Engage further, share others' content, comment on it, congratulate them on achievements, etc. It does not need to be excessive, or invasive, but you should make an honest effort to enter the conversation, to remain relevant, visible, and engaged.

The key point to remember is that having lots of contacts is helpful but not sufficient for success. Your success will depend on how you use your network, and you'll need to add value to it by contributing conversation, content, and insight before you can extract value from it in the form of job opportunities and referrals. Building the network and your value to it does not happen overnight. It takes a significant amount of time and effort, but you'll be able to reap benefits from it now, and likely for a very long time afterwards.

While all social media platforms can be useful for networking, LinkedIn has emerged as the Facebook for professional networking. With LinkedIn you can develop a large number of contacts by linking electronically in your own personal network. Many people have several hundred connections through LinkedIn, and some even have over 1,000 connections. There are also many subgroups appearing on LinkedIn such as employees from a particular company or industry, and groups of alumni from specific colleges and universities. This networking process is gaining wide acceptance, and many companies are now advertising openings on LinkedIn, making it a viable resource for job search. As stated in Chapter 3, how your profiles represent you on all social media platforms is critical, but having and maintaining a living, active LinkedIn profile is essential. With that in mind, please take the time needed to complete the following exercise.

EXERCISE 1

You should now have a completed resume which provides the basic information needed to create your LinkedIn profile. You will also need a professional photo (headshot) for use on your LinkedIn page. Go to linkedin.com to create your page, or update it using your new resume, and start "linking" to people you know and requesting introductions to people who can possibly help you with your search!

## EXERCISE 2

All social media platforms are now being used by employers to determine the character of a candidate and if they are a likely fit for a job. Take the time right now to thoroughly inspect your social media profiles, posts, and pictures (on Instagram, Twitter, Snapchat, Facebook, etc.) and remove anything that might send the wrong message to an employer. Cross check your security settings as well to protect yourself from unwanted tags or associations.

## NETWORKING AND YOUR BIRKMAN RESULTS

Before moving to the final assignment in this chapter, take a few minutes to review some of your Birkman results in light of the networking process, what is required to network effectively, and how both may make you feel or react.

## EXERCISE 3

**Please refer back to a Birkman report referenced earlier in the book, "How You Handle Other People, Section 2: Your less effective approach."**

Take a moment to re-read each of the statements in this section slowly, considering how these tendencies might impact your ability to network effectively. Record your thoughts below.

## EXERCISE 4

**Please refer to "How You Handle Other People, Section 1: When you are at your best."**

Take a moment to consider each of the statements in context of developing a strategy for networking that will play to your strengths. In the space below write down at least 5 words that describe your networking strengths.

## GETTING STARTED

Finally, this chapter will have little impact on your search if you don't start using the information immediately. Ideally you'll have a working list of 100+ networking contacts, but for now, a list of 10 will get you moving in the right direction. In the space below list 10 people you know who may have professional contacts, particularly in the companies or organizations that interest you. Once you have completed the list, follow the instructions provided at the end of the chapter to begin expanding and utilizing this network.

|  | NAME | COMPANY | EMAIL | CELL |
|---|---|---|---|---|
| 1 | | | | |
| 2 | | | | |
| 3 | | | | |
| 4 | | | | |
| 5 | | | | |
| 6 | | | | |
| 7 | | | | |
| 8 | | | | |
| 9 | | | | |
| 10 | | | | |

## WHAT'S NEXT?

To utilize this networking list effectively, do the following within the next 5 days:

1. Check to see if the contacts listed have LinkedIn accounts. If so, ask to "connect" to them.

2. Email or call them and let them know you are in the market and inform them of your specific career objective and your unique qualifications.

3. Ask them for an informational interview.

4. Email them your resume, if they ask for one.

5. Ask for additional names of individuals they know who may be able to assist you.

You are on your way! Continue these steps with every new contact and your network will grow fast. The faster it grows, the sooner you will find yourself employed and starting the career of your dreams.

# BE INTENTIONAL

- STAY IN TOUCH WITH OLD FRIENDS AND MAKE NEW ONES.
- LISTEN, LISTEN, LISTEN.
- CONTACT 3-4 PROFESSIONALS IN A FIELD THAT INTERESTS YOU AND REQUEST AN INFORMATIONAL INTERVIEW.
- BE CAREFUL WHOSE NAME YOU USE AS A REFERENCE.
- ABOVE ALL, YOUR CREDIBILITY IS YOUR MOST IMPORTANT ASSET.
- LEARN FROM OTHERS.

# CHAPTER 9

# Defining the Search Parameters

OUTCOMES:

## I WILL DEVELOP AN UNDERSTANDING OF THE FACTORS THAT WILL DRIVE MY SEARCH, INCLUDING LOCATION, FUNCTION, AND INDUSTRY OR SECTOR.

If you have made it this far in the book, you have clearly done significant self-reflection and work towards understanding who you are, your strengths and accomplishments, and your general career direction. In addition, you now have a resume and LinkedIn profile polished and ready. Now it is time to determine what job search parameters you will set in light of the current marketplace and your unique desires and restrictions.

There are three key factors that guide both the internship and job search processes: location, job function, and industry. For most people, one of these factors is much more important that the other two, but for some all three are equally important. Only you can make that determination for your search, and many factors contribute to the varied weights of these factors.

If you are single, location may currently not be a factor, but it might become a major factor once you are married, cohabitating, or have children. Job function is often the main driver for those with skills-based degrees or experience, like nurses, engineers, teachers, or law enforcement officers. Others may be more open regarding what they do, but know they want to be in a specific industry (tourism, healthcare, sports and athletics, etc.). Often the industry preference is driven by what interests someone on a personal level, so be mindful of this as you work through the exercises in this chapter.

The following exercises are designed to guide you as you define and fine-tune your specific search parameters along with the associated weight of each one. Please seriously consider the questions asked, and take whatever time is necessary to provide your answers, as they will guide the rest of the search process.

## EXERCISE 1

LOCATION: Do you have geographical limitations, or are you free to move anywhere for the right opportunity?

☐ I am free to move anywhere          ☐ I have geographical limitations

If you indicated you have limitations, please complete the following:

I need to be within miles ____ of this location: _____

OR...   I would prefer to, or need to, live in one of the following cities:
1)
2)
3)

OR...   I would prefer to, or need to, live in the following regions/country/province:

## EXERCISE 2

JOB FUNCTION: Based on the work you did in Chapter 4 related to your Career Directions, what are the three to five job functions you will target? Prioritize them below with #1 being your top preference.

1.

2.

3.

4.

5.

## EXERCISE 3

Based on all you have learned about yourself so far, what industry(ies) or business sector(s) are you most attracted to at this point (e.g., law enforcement, healthcare, K-12 education, tourism, media, agribusiness, entertainment, sports operations, etc.)? List 5 in rank order.

1.
2.
3.
4.
5.

## EXERCISE 4

Based on your answers in the previous exercises, you have all the information needed to record your search parameters in summary form. This information will drive your research, your conversations, your networking, and your interviewing. In the space below, record your answers creating a concise Parameters Summary. You will calculate the "Importance Value" requested once this portion of the exercise is complete.

## JOB SEARCH PARAMETERS SUMMARY

My primary geographic targets are _____ .

(Importance _____ )

My primary job function targets are _____ .

(Importance _____ )

My industry or business sector targets are _____ .

(Importance _____ )

Finally, you must determine the importance, or weight, of these factors to determine how to define and develop your marketing plan. With 100 being the total value available, please assign a value to each of the 3 factors listed above. You may divide them equally (33.3 each) or you may have 1 that is the lead driver with 80 points and the other two factor at 10 each. There is no wrong answer, but determining the right answer for you is critical.

Now you have the parameters to begin your search. In the next chapter you will use this information to develop a marketing plan.

# BE INTENTIONAL

- BE HONEST WITH YOURSELF ABOUT THE IMPORTANCE OF LOCATION.
- KNOW WHAT YOU WANT, WHAT YOU NEED, AND LEARN TO TELL THE DIFFERENCE.
- REMEMBER YOUR PRIORITIES.

# CHAPTER 10

# Developing Your Marketing Plan

OUTCOMES:

## I WILL CREATE A STRUCTURED, WELL-THOUGHT-OUT MARKETING PLAN AND UNDERSTAND MY TOP TARGETS AND THE BEST WAYS TO ENHANCE MY OPPORTUNITIES WITHIN THOSE ORGANIZATIONS.

At this point, you have defined your strengths and accomplishments, you have a resume and a LinkedIn profile established, and, thanks to the Birkman Method®, you have a better understanding of how this search process is likely to impact you, and where you may struggle. Finally, you understand the importance of networking and have assessed the market and your specific search parameters. With all of that in place, it is time to begin the marketing process and get your search underway. For this to be effective you must fully embrace the concept that "you are the product."

You must approach the marketing process with this mindset. As with any marketing initiative for a specific product, this will require that you develop a plan you intend to follow. For many, this can be the hardest part of the process. It requires a systematic approach, similar to formal project management in a corporate environment. This approach is necessary because it allows you to set goals and success criteria, track your steps, and measure your progress.

## DEVELOPING THE PLAN

In the previous chapter you determined the geographic parameters for your search. Please review these specifics and write them here:

- Search Locations (s): _____
- In the previous chapter you also determined what industry(s) were of most interest to you. Please list those again here: _____
- Finally, as a part of your work in the previous chapter, you fine-tuned the specific jobs or functions that you should target. Please list those here: _____

## EXERCISE 1

With these specifics mind, it is time to develop a target list of 10 companies or organizations in your target location(s) that fit your industry preference(s) and have positions in line with your chosen job or function. We will refer to this as your Top 10 List. You will use Table 10.1 to keep track of your targets.

This will require research and will take some time, so do not rush the process. Take whatever time is needed to develop a relevant list from which to work. The following resources will be useful as you refine this list:

Hoovers.com
Careerinfonet.org
Glassdoor.com
Vault.com
Career-advice.monster.com
LinkedIn.com
Indeed.com

## TARGET ORGANIZATIONS (TABLE 10.1)

|    | INDUSTRY | LOCATION | COMPANY/ORGANIZATION |
|----|----------|----------|----------------------|
| 1  |          |          |                      |
| 2  |          |          |                      |
| 3  |          |          |                      |
| 4  |          |          |                      |
| 5  |          |          |                      |
| 6  |          |          |                      |
| 7  |          |          |                      |
| 8  |          |          |                      |
| 9  |          |          |                      |
| 10 |          |          |                      |

Now that you have established your Top 10 List, it is time to revisit the networking exercise on page 65. Are any of the people listed on your previous networking list employed at any of the targets you listed above? If so, list them again in Table 10.2.

# NETWORKING RESOURCES (TABLE 10.2)

| NETWORKING NAME | TARGET COMPANY | THEIR ROLE | CONTACT INFO |
|---|---|---|---|
| | | | |
| | | | |
| | | | |
| | | | |
| | | | |
| | | | |
| | | | |
| | | | |
| | | | |
| | | | |
| | | | |
| | | | |
| | | | |

Assuming that you did not fill up the chart with networking contacts you have already identified, it is now time to expand your networking list. To do this, you will need to use your LinkedIn account, and other social media options to search for contacts within these companies and organizations. You will also need to talk to friends and family members to source additional names.

Your entire network should be aware of your target list and should assist you in adding more names to it. Also, you will continue to add to this list as you speak with people personally about your interest in their company or organization. You may choose to develop a spreadsheet for use as you continue to expand this list. Either way, please understand that this list should expand regularly as you advance through your search.

## TOTAL PACKAGE

Congratulations! You have completed all of the preparation work and have compiled a Personal Marketing Plan with the following components:

- Resume
- LinkedIn Profile
- Target List
- Networking list

Now it's time to put all of this preparation to work.

# BE INTENTIONAL

- DO THOROUGH RESEARCH ABOUT A COMPANY OR ORGANIZATION BEFORE YOU ADD THEM TO YOUR TARGET LIST.
- NOT ALL GOOD OPPORTUNITIES ARE WITH COMPANIES WHOSE NAMES YOU KNOW.
- JUST BECAUSE YOU DON'T KNOW THE NAME OF A COMPANY DOESN'T MEAN YOU CAN'T HAVE A GREAT CAREER THERE!

# CHAPTER 11

# Implementing Your Search

OUTCOMES:

## I WILL BEGIN AN ACTIVE JOB OR INTERNSHIP SEARCH USING THE TOOLS, MARKETING MATERIALS, AND LISTS ALREADY DEVELOPED.

You've worked hard developing your marketing materials, your plan, and your networking list. Now it's time to put the plan into action. You will be implementing your plan utilizing several strategies simultaneously. These include:

1. Conducting informational interviews
2. Searching for open positions on company websites
3. Using search engines
4. Contacting employment agencies or headhunters
5. Utilizing your college or university's career center

## INFORMATIONAL INTERVIEWS

One of the most important parts of the search process is arranging for informational interviews. These are conversations with individuals who have some affiliation with one of your target companies/organizations. The purpose of these conversations IS NOT TO ASK FOR A JOB. It is to learn more about the industry, the company or the function within both.

This is an essential component of your search, allowing you to determine if you truly want to work for a particular employer, within a specific industry, or in certain job. The following questions are examples of things you could ask during one of these conversations.

1. Can you tell me about the advantages of working with your employer or within your industry?
2. Are there unique challenges facing your employer where my skills and experience might be of use?
3. Why did you decide to work here?

4. What attracted you to this industry?

5. What advice do you have for me as I try to gain employment here or in this industry?

6. Do you know of anyone else I should speak with to learn more as I continue my search?

Please note: You absolutely MUST ask #6. You should leave every informational interview with the name of someone else you can call to arrange another informational interview.

Why is this so important?

1. You must continue to widen your network

2. You want to be "top of mind" for a large number of people so that when they do have an opportunity available they think of you BEFORE THE JOB IS EVEN POSTED.

The more informational interviews you can schedule, the more successful your search will be. The more people you talk to, the more people know who you are and understand your career objectives. To facilitate this process, we suggest that you set "contact targets" for each week. A sample "Contact/Application Tracking Sheet" is provided on the following page. This tracking sheet can help you keep track of your progress. We strongly encourage you to use this sheet, or one like it, to make sure you are using your time in the most effective and efficient ways.

## EMPLOYER WEBSITES

Although the process of applying for positions on a company's website can be extremely frustrating, you simply must go through the process. You must regularly search the sites of the organizations on your Top 10 List and continuously apply, formally, on the websites. Why is this so important? In short: it's company policy. Even if you become a referral for a position that is open and posted on the company website, you are most likely not going to land an interview if you are not "in their system." With this in mind, get organized, follow a set schedule, set targets, and apply, apply, apply! Keep calling, keep talking, and keep asking for someone else's name!

However, clicking "submit" should not be the end of the process. Crosscheck your networking list and contact anyone affiliated with the company to let them know that you have just applied for a job or internship. They may be in a position to "put in a good word for you," or formally refer you. When you apply for a job or internship, the outcome you want is an interview. Work both angles, the formal process and the networking process, to better your chances of landing that interview! Table 11.1 will help you structure your approach to this process. It also will help you track your networking contacts, as described in the previous section.

# TABLE 11.1 CONTACT/APPLICATION TRACKING SHEET

|  | WEEK 1 | WEEK 2 | WEEK 3 | WEEK 4 | WEEK 5 | WEEK 6 | WEEK 7 | WEEK 8 |
|---|---|---|---|---|---|---|---|---|
| NETWORKING CONTACTS TARGET |  |  |  |  |  |  |  |  |
| NETWORKING CONTACTS MADE |  |  |  |  |  |  |  |  |
| INFORMATIONAL INTERVIEW TARGET |  |  |  |  |  |  |  |  |
| INFORMATIONAL INTERVIEWS |  |  |  |  |  |  |  |  |
| COMPLETED |  |  |  |  |  |  |  |  |
| TOP 10 WEBSITE APPLICATIONS |  |  |  |  |  |  |  |  |
| TARGET |  |  |  |  |  |  |  |  |
| TOP 10 APPLICATIONS COMPLETED |  |  |  |  |  |  |  |  |
| NETWORKING CONTACTS INFORMED |  |  |  |  |  |  |  |  |
| OF APPLICATIONS |  |  |  |  |  |  |  |  |
| JOB INTERVIEWS SCHEDULED |  |  |  |  |  |  |  |  |
| JOB INTERVIEWS COMPLETED |  |  |  |  |  |  |  |  |

## SEARCH ENGINES

Most employers utilize large search engines like Monster.com, Careerbuilder.com and Indeed.com. To hedge your search effectively, you must be engaged with these sites. Keep the following in mind as you create accounts on these engines and submit your marketing materials.

- Be vigilant about ensuring your information is up-to-date and current. You can't post a resume once and never return to update it or confirm its validity.
- Utilize the search agent options available on each site to provide notices via email or sent to your phone when a position is posted that fits your parameter. This "push" notification is much more efficient than manually searching the site every day.
- Focus on the companies you have listed in your Top 10 list, but be open to expanding your list if you find opportunities on these sites that interest you.

Finally, just as with the company websites, if you do find opportunities and complete applications through these sites remember to utilize your network to determine if you know someone within the organization. If so, you should contact them and let them know that you have completed an online application via this method.

Currently, the best large search engines include:
- Monster.com
- Careerbuilder.com
- Indeed.com
- Simplyhired.com
- LinkedIn.com

## COLLEGE OR UNIVERSITY CAREER CENTER

If you are a college student in the internship or job market you should contact your school's career center during your junior year, at the latest. They will work with you to prepare your marketing materials, assess your options, and assist you in preparing for the interview and negotiating process. What is equally as valuable, however, is the employer network available to you as a student. If you are a recent alum this is also the most valuable aspect of reconnecting with your career center.

In some sense, employers that regularly recruit at a specific school already view the candidates from that school as referrals. The programs of study and the career coaching are known entities to the recruiters and they have placed their faith in both when committing to recruit or screen resumes. They trust the school and its personnel so you would be foolish to not utilize this network.

Most likely you will be required to have a resume approved and create an account within the school's online recruiting program. This becomes another search engine for you and you should treat it as you would the large engines discussed earlier in this chapter.

Finally, utilizing your school's resources, which might include access to a LinkedIn or Facebook alumni groups, gives you access to a vital networking option: your school's alumni. Alumni are typically very receptive to assisting students from their school or fellow alumni, so don't be hesitant to ask for their help.

So now you have the materials, you are prepared to interview, you have a plan, and you know the job search processes. It's time to start your search. Get started today!

## BE INTENTIONAL

- MOMENTUM AND PROGRESS ARE SO IMPORTANT BECAUSE THEY WILL KEEP YOU MOVING IN THE INTENDED DIRECTION.
- TAKE THE TIME TO SET UP YOUR PROFILES ON THE SEARCH ENGINES THOROUGHLY THE FIRST TIME.
- FOLLOW UP, AND THEN FOLLOW UP MORE.

# CHAPTER 12

# Understanding the Sourcing & Screening Process

OUTCOMES:

## I WILL BETTER UNDERSTAND THE MIND OF THE RECRUITER AND HAVE ADDITIONAL KNOWLEDGE AND INSIGHT THAT WILL HELP ME NAVIGATE THE SEARCH PROCESS.

When turnover occurs in an organization, meaning someone has left an existing position, it is not immediately assumed that the position will be filled. Initially, the job will be assessed to determine if it can be eliminated or if the duties can be divided up among other existing positions. The target is to save money, and all companies are attempting to manage their resources in a cost effective manner. If the position survives this process, and it is determined that a hire must be made, the job description, job requirements, and compensation are evaluated to make sure that the recruiters and candidates have a clear understanding of the qualifications for the job. Once this has occurred, the recruiter can begin sourcing for the job. "Sourcing" is the human resources process of seeking qualified candidates.

Something similar happens when new work is added within an organization. New work can develop when there is an increased demand for the products or services provided by the organization, when new products or services are introduced, and/or when new technology or methods are integrated into the organization. In these cases, a similar evaluation is conducted of the duties that need to be performed. If it is determined that a new person must be hired, the human resources office will develop a job description, determine job requirements and compensation for the job, and begin sourcing for the position.

## INTERNAL CANDIDATES

Typically, the company will seek internal candidates first. Most organizations have an internal job posting process, allowing interested and qualified internal candidates to bid for the open job. Qualified candidates are interviewed, with the best candidate selected to fill the opening. Considering internal candidates in this fashion creates good morale and commitment in the organization.

## REFERRALS

If there are no internal candidates, the organization will look for external candidates. A company's first resource is usually their "hot file" of resumes. This file will generally consist of referrals from employees or other sources, and candidates seen for other openings that have good general experience for the organization. Many companies will electronically scan the resumes of these potential candidates into a system where they can be retrieved by entering job specifications. It is not uncommon for an organization to seek out a candidate that has been in the hot file for 6 months or more. As discussed in Chapter 8, jobs filled in this manner never get to the market (known as silent job market), and filling them is virtually free to the company.

If the hot file doesn't produce a candidate, the company will seek other types of referrals. Similar to the hot file, there is no additional cost for candidates who are referrals. Frequently, the human resources department will circulate or post a list of open jobs so current employees can generate referrals. As discussed in Chapter 8, this is why it is crucial that you constantly work your network within the organizations on your target list!

Obviously, organizations view referrals in a very favorable manner. There is very little cost associated with a referral and they generally come with a perception of a positive performance outcome (employees will not refer someone who will reflect poorly on them). Another positive aspect of sourcing referrals centers on the candidate's view of the organization. In general, the organization can assume that the referring employee has briefed the candidate about the company in a favorable fashion and provided an overview to assist the candidate in preparing for an interview. Keep in mind that the cost of advertising open jobs, college recruiting, attending job fairs, and using employment agencies is very expensive for companies, sometimes running as high as 25 percent of the candidate's starting salary.

FOR THIS REASON, YOU CAN EXPECT THAT SEEKING A REFERRAL WILL ALWAYS BE THE FIRST SOURCING METHOD USED BY ORGANIZATIONS, WHICH IS WHY THE NETWORKING PROCESS CONTINUES TO BE YOUR MOST IMPORTANT LINE OF ATTACK IN YOUR SEARCH.

## CASE 1: A SIGNIFICANT SAVINGS FOR A COMPANY WITH A REFERRAL COMPARED TO NORMAL RECRUITING SOURCES

The recruiter for a software company had the assignment to hire 3 new software engineers to help with growing volume from new customers. The average salary for the position was $110,000. The company's website was not pulling candidates. The recruiter checked the costs of recruiting sources and found that an employment agency would charge 25 percent of the starting salary, or $82,000, to fill the 3 positions. The right kinds of ads in publications and online sites would cost a minimum $20,000. He decided to post the job internally to seek referrals. He offered an incentive of $1,000 for any software engineer referred and hired, payable after the new employee completed 6 months of service. In the end, the total recruiting cost was $3,000, a substantial savings over conventional recruiting sources.

Many companies have instituted bonus or incentive programs for employees who make referrals. These incentives are usually cash, credits to buy company products, or credits to buy products from a premium catalog. Companies are also reaching out to customers, suppliers and others—trade associations, college professors, and friends. Referrals save companies large amounts of money and most of the positions filled by referrals never appear on the open job market.

## ORGANIZATION WEBSITE POSTINGS

If the referral process is unsuccessful, the most common next step is for the organization to use its website for recruiting. Next to a referral, use of the company website is the least expensive approach to recruiting and sources. Over time, company websites have become very sophisticated recruiting tools. Keep in mind that most all companies will list middle-level and lower-level openings on their websites, but they do not always list upper-level jobs.

They will generally post the open job title, a job description, the physical location of the job, and any special requirements of the job. Some employers will have a sign-in procedure for candidates to submit their resumes online and they may require the candidate to fill in a formal employment application and/or attest that their resume is factually correct (if the candidate is hired and subsequent lies are found, the candidate can be terminated). Additionally, some companies will require an online aptitude test, and possibly a brief background check to further qualify the candidate.

## CASE 2: PARTIAL BACKGROUND CHECK AT TIME OF RESUME SUBMISSION

A major retail chain does a brief background check on any resume that passes their initial screening process. All candidates sign a release that permits a background check. The retail chain has major concerns with any candidate that has a conviction for a felony, or that has severe credit problems. The issue is theft. The data indicates that employee theft is on the rise, and they want to eliminate candidates that have any potential for theft. Their online application system has a direct interface with a large background checking organization, so checking these factors is a simple process. In almost all cases these types of background checks can be performed with online resources. When the background check turns up a problem, the candidate is eliminated. For successful candidates, a full background check is completed later, before an employment offer is finalized.

## COLLEGE RECRUITING

Most major organizations seek a close relationship with a few colleges or universities that produce qualified candidates for their particular business. It is also important that graduates from a particular school have proven to be successful in their organization. Often the employer will provide financial support to these schools, participate on advisory boards, and serve as guest lecturers in classes.

Many colleges have a career management office that serves as the primary interface with outside organizations interested in hiring students. These college offices will work with students to help them improve their resumes, interviewing skills, and their job search capability. Usually students upload their resumes into a system that employers can access and post open jobs. The career services office will also coordinate company recruiting on campus.

When companies prepare to recruit on campus, they can post their open jobs and review the resumes of interested students in advance. Companies will also host "open house" meetings for students. Keep in mind that every meeting between a company representative and a candidate is part of the screening process. Companies are constantly observing how a candidate handles himself, how he is dressed and groomed, and how he communicates.

Companies will use this same process when they recruit at trade or technical schools.

## CASE 3: MISSING OUT ON AN OPPORTUNITY

A university professor invited a guest speaker from the human resources department of a major retail organization to present the company's recruiting process to the class. The guest lecturer mentioned to the professor that she would accept resumes from the class members at the end of the lecture. The professor let the class know in advance that the company would accept resumes after the class. During the class, it was clear that the company representative was observing the class during her presentation. She was looking for class participation, engagement, and how students were dressed. At the end of the class, each student who wanted to submit a resume had a brief period of time to speak to the company representative. She evaluated how they communicated, presented their capabilities, were groomed and dressed, and what they knew about the company. After collecting a dozen resumes, the corporate representative sat down and evaluated everyone based on their skills, the brief presentation of their resumes, their participation in class, and the ways they were dressed and groomed. She stated that anytime she is involved in a class, open house, or job fair, she is always evaluating everyone she meets as a potential candidate. She added that she expected people who want to be candidates to realize that in almost every situation, she is considering anyone she meets as a potential candidate.

Generally, during the college recruiting process, recruiters typically gain only a superficial knowledge of potential candidates (unless there is time for a full interview). Consequently, the candidates that are moved along in the process are those who make a good initial impression, and not necessarily those who will be the best employees.

## NEVER UNDERESTIMATE THE POWER OF THE FIRST IMPRESSION!

### JOB FAIRS

Many colleges, universities, and outside organizations sponsor job or career fairs. A fair is an opportunity for candidates to meet numerous employers gathered in one location who are looking for job candidates and open jobs to fill. For the employer it is an opportunity to meet numerous candidates in one location, allowing them to potentially source multiple candidates at once.

Sometimes companies pay a fee to participate. This is particularly true of high tech and other occupations where candidates are scarce. Even if there is no fee for the company, there are other costs associated with a job fair. Paid staff must attend the event, which includes travel and lodging expenses, fair site expenses, and some miscellaneous expenses. The return on their investment is based on the number of people they hire from the job fair, which will depend on their ability to assess candidate quality after only speaking to them briefly.

To increase their odds of learning as much as possible in the short time available at these events, they often inquire, "tell me about yourself" when a candidate approaches their table. The next step for a candidate is contingent upon how well she answers this question. A candidate needs to describe her skills and how she can make an excellent contribution to the company in a very brief time period. If she can present herself effectively, she will be screened in, and scheduled for an interview at a later date.

### ADVERTISING

Once upon a time, the most common place to look for a listing of job openings was in the newspaper. For the most part, those days are gone. Print advertising has been declining rapidly in recent years. Although there are still some print ads in local markets, and on a national scale with The Wall Street Journal and The New York Times, most employment advertising has moved to online sources. For those employers who do still utilize print ads, there is a significant cost. These ads can cost thousands of dollars for national publications or hundreds of dollars for local ads.

There are a growing number of online sites where companies can advertise their open jobs by posting them on the site for a fee, based on the number of ads and the length of time the ad(s) run.

These ads generally cost in the low hundreds for each advertisement. The sites include monster. com, careerbuilder.com, indeed.org, and others mentioned in Chapter 11. Please review these sites and make sure you have created the appropriate accounts and profiles.

## TEMPORARY HELP AGENCIES

Companies generally use temporary help agencies when they have a short-term need for an employee to complete a specific job. They are often used as a probationary period for a potential new employee, a trial period. In this situation, the company has no obligation to hire if the situation does not work out. In addition, during the temporary employment there are typically no company benefits, which is an added savings for the company. Since the individual is actually employed by the temporary agency, terminating the employee is done by the agency, not the company, which is also a benefit to the company's brand as an employer.

> ### CASE 4: HOW COMPANIES PAY TEMPORARY HELP AGENCIES
> A temporary agency may bill a company $20 per hour for a temporary employee. The temporary employee may receive $15 per hour, and the remaining $5 goes to the temporary agency for payroll tax and other costs, and profit. (This is an over simplification to show in general how these systems work.) Companies are always looking at their temporary employees as potential full-time regular employees. If the temporary employee does a good job in their temporary situation, they can be considered for regular full-time positions.

## EMPLOYMENT AGENCIES

Traditional employment agencies provide a fee-based service to companies. They will recruit and screen candidates for specific open jobs and their average fees to the company will run 20 percent to 25 percent of the employee's starting salary. Employment agencies often run ads to obtain candidates, and most have extensive files of applicants. Companies will frequently use employment agencies for hard-to-fill openings, or where lower cost recruiting sources haven't worked. Frequently, employment agencies may specialize in key occupational areas and become very good resources for companies and candidates. Sometimes companies can negotiate reduced fees by offering a significant number of open jobs to an agency on an exclusive basis.

## EXECUTIVE SEARCH

Executive search firms find senior job candidates for companies. Their targets are generally senior executives who are gainfully employed and not necessarily looking for a job. The search firms will do research on companies and network to find candidates, and most search firms have extensive libraries on corporate information and key candidates. Companies will generally contract with

executive search firms for a fee of 30 percent to 35 percent of the first year's compensation plus expenses for screening and interviewing candidates. The company may specify target companies that would provide good candidates. The search firm is obligated to present qualified candidates to earn its fee, regardless of whether or not the company hires one of the candidates. This recruiting resource is a last resort for companies and only used for senior-level jobs, due to the expense.

## SCREENING RESUMES

All of the aforementioned sourcing methods result in resumes that must be evaluated and screened. It is imperative that you understand this screening process to best position yourself against competing candidates.

The purpose of this screening process is to review resumes critically to match backgrounds to open job qualifications. The desired outcome of this process is to identify a workable number of candidates who will be evaluated further with the most successful candidates being interviewed in person.

If a small number of resumes are to be screened, a human resources representative will typically go through them and screen in qualified candidates. Some resumes of unqualified candidates, who may be qualified for other positions within the company, are generally held in an electronic hot file. These resumes may be accessed for other open jobs at a later date.

Major companies seeking a large number of candidates to fill open jobs may screen resumes electronically. They use scanning systems that can identify key words or factors in a resume that are qualifications of the job. Such things as technical qualifications, specific experience, education, certifications, supervisory requirements, etc., can be programmed into the scanning system. Resumes that appear to reflect none of the required qualifications are screened out. Depending on other factors on the resume, a few may be placed in a hot file for future openings. The objective in this whole process is to find resumes of individuals who appears to be the most qualified candidates for the open position with the objective of moving forward in the process, most likely to the interview stage.

## TELEPHONE OR WEB-BASED VISUAL SCREENS

Typically, candidates who are screened into the process following a resume review will complete a telephone or Skype/FaceTime interview prior to being invited to an on-site interview. These interviews are usually scripted to some extent by the company, to include behavioral questions involving duties and competencies required in the job. There will also be technical questions about the specific job. Often, candidates are asked the same questions as others who are competing for the same position. After all candidates are interviewed in this manner, evaluations are made and the best candidates are invited to a face-to-face interview.

The candidate is not only being judged on verbal responses but also on appearance and emotional intelligence. A candidate must be prepared for this type of interview by following the steps outlined in Chapter 13.

# BE INTENTIONAL

- TECHNOLOGY IS BEING USED MORE AND MORE IN THE RECRUITING PROCESS. BE AWARE OF A SPECIFIC COMPANY'S RECRUITING TECHNIQUES BEFORE YOU INTERVIEW WITH THEM!
- REMEMBER THAT RECRUITERS' JOBS ARE TO FIND THE BEST CANDIDATES FOR THEIR OPEN POSITIONS, NOT TO MAKE YOU FEEL GOOD ABOUT YOURSELF.

# CHAPTER 13
# Preparing for a Specific Interview

OUTCOME:

## I WILL HAVE A STRATEGY FOR PREPARING FOR A SPECIFIC INTERVIEW AND I WILL KNOW WHAT WILL BE EXPECTED IN THE INTERVIEW PROCESS.

In Chapter 7 you should have completed a thorough process of interview preparation that focused on your experiences, skills, and talents, in a general sense. This chapter will discuss preparing for a specific interview, which will not be effective if you do not remember the details of your overall interviewing preparation; therefore, if it has been awhile since you read Chapter 7 please spend a few minutes reviewing the information before proceeding.

Now, it is time to discuss the very tactical approach to preparing for a specific interview. In general, assuming that you are completely familiar with your strengths, weaknesses, talents, and gifts, and you have developed a series of "stories" related to your past experience and accomplishments, there are two things you must focus on to prepare for a scheduled interview: 1) the specific job description, and 2) the current condition of the company or organization with which you are interviewing.

## ANALYZING THE JOB
Never underestimate the importance of a thorough analysis of a job description or posting. Each one provides clues as to what the recruiter is looking for in a candidate, and what they may ask you. To get a feel for how to conduct this analysis, please read the following Job Posting and then answer the questions asked.

## MARKETING COORDINATOR POSITION

*Available in Tampa, Florida*

As a Marketing Coordinator you will work closely with our Marketing Directors and Managers to gain valuable experience executing various direct mail and digital, email campaigns. You will be responsible for independently analyzing prospect and customer data; preparing routine reports and correspondence; and administratively aiding in the collection and presentation of data.

- Facilitates marketing campaigns ensuring timely and quality implementation of all related tasks.
- Generates reports with order information and transfers data into marketing analyses.
- Maintains spreadsheets and performs cost analysis of marketing efforts.
- Develops analyses to track the performance of marketing efforts to prospects.
- Manages and maintains product data within company systems.
- Conducts market research to assist in the development and execution of marketing plan objectives.
- Interacts and corresponds with members of the sales, customer service, and editorial teams.

## EXERCISE 1

In Chapter 5, the various Core Competencies sought by most employers were listed, along with questions for you to answer regarding your own skill level. Those competencies are listed below. Circle three to five that you believe would be required to do this job effectively and with excellence:

Critical Thinking/Problem Solving

Teamwork/Collaboration

Professionalism/Work Ethic

Oral/Written Communication

Leadership

Digital Technology

Career Management

Global/Intercultural Fluency

## CUSTOMER ORIENTATION

Now, returning once again to Chapter 5, review your answers to the questions following each of the competencies you circled. Why? Because if these are the competencies the recruiter is looking for, they will certainly want you to discuss your skills in these areas. You must be ready to prove you have what they are looking for if you expect to be hired!

Now, go back to Chapter 7 and review the STAR stories you developed, which focused on the specific accomplishments from your past. Which ones would be most appropriate to prove the competencies you circled above? Are there others you could prepare for this specific interview?

Bottom line? You must determine, by reading the job description and posting, what they are likely looking for and you must be ready to prove you have it! Proving it is essential. You should never just say "yes" to a question about whether or not you have a specific ability. You should ALWAYS give an example – tell your story!

One final point on the job analysis process: In addition to reading the descriptions and postings, if you have access to someone within the organization, try to speak with them about the job and what they believe is the most important trait(s) of the right candidates. This will give you one more layer of information for use in preparing!

## UNDERSTANDING THE EMPLOYER/COMPANY/ORGANIZATION

Understanding the current climate in which an employer/company lives is vital. Their current stressors and challenges are likely foremost on their minds, and an appreciation of the impact on both the company and the individual will go a long way in pushing you to the top of the hiring list. You should already be engaging in some "due diligence" ahead of your interview by researching the position and seeking to understand the company, its culture, and employees ahead of your first meeting. You can extend this process by doing your own social listening, using their digital footprint to gauge what they value most, and then determining how you should position yourself to increase your chances of getting their offer.

By investing some time and effort you can go through a firm's social media presence (LinkedIn, Facebook, Twitter, Instagram, etc.) and take note of their updates, what they choose to share or comment on, and the extent of their activity in general (do they post at all, a little, or a lot). Take note of who they engage with, as well as what they share from other sources. At the very least, this research should give you an idea of how they compete in the marketplace and what sort of value they see themselves as providing to their customers. At this point you should ask yourself how you can contribute to this strategy, and what value you bring to the company – this will be something you'll want to get across during your interview since you are trying to place yourself as the best "product" for them.

With a little more digging you might find other important pieces of information that can be used during the interview. Maybe the company is expanding into a new location, or into a new country. Maybe the president of the company made a recent announcement or statement that impacts the position for which you are interviewing. All of these examples lead to great questions during the interview. For instance, "How will the expansion into XYZ impact my potential duties?" or "With the company moving into XYZ, are there opportunities for me to engage/interact with those managers and learn from their experiences?" or "Considering Mr. CEO's statement last Tuesday, how do you see the growth of the division we're talking about?," etc.

In fact, with enough time and energy, you can employ this approach for the firm's competitors as well to get a more complete understanding of everything the firm is facing.

Whether you choose to engage in social listening or not and how much depends on the type of position you are interviewing for, and who you expect to be interviewing with, since some questions might be appropriate for managers with more intimate knowledge of day-to-day operations. However, the advantage in the approach is clear: demonstrate knowledge about the company, demonstrate interest, and further set yourself apart from other candidates.

Additional social listening can happen in professional social platforms like LinkedIn, where you can turn your focus away from the firm itself and towards its current and former employees. You can use the information contained here to understand the background of their employees or to gauge the common skillsets that lead to, or arise from, employment in the firm. Does it look like a good match from your perspective? Are you bringing something novel or unique to this position? You certainly would want to bring up any of these points in an interview to further highlight the value you potentially bring to the company. Along similar lines, you can attempt to determine an average tenure time for employees in that company. There's a good chance that a company that does not keep employees for more than a few months at a time has some internal/culture problems that are not immediately visible from outside or from asking questions during the interview process. This sort of information could be invaluable to you when choosing the right job offer.

As you do this research and social listening, you will need to track what you learn in some meaningful way so you will be fully prepared as you go into the interview. The planning guides that follow provide basic models for learning about an employer's business and uncovering ways you can best meet their specific needs. Set them up on your laptop computer, in file folders, loose-leaf binders, or in any manner that best suits your working habits. They are meant only to help you get started thinking, learning, and growing with the employer. Please add to the categories and develop your own planning guides.

## EMPLOYER GUIDES FOR JOB INTERVIEW PREPARATION

### Overall Information

Customer Profile:

Alliances:

Customer's Vision/Overall Goals:

Key Departments/Services:

Key People/Contacts:

Key Competition:

Customer's Major Business Issues/Challenges:

### Sales Information

Customer's Target Market/Demographics:

Customer's Competitive Advantages:

Products:

Competitive Products:

Major Supporters for this Customer:

Opportunities and Any Obstacles for Major Product Success:

Factors for Needs of The Customer:

Product Benefits of Priority to their Customers:

### Needs of their Customer:

Value-Added Services the Company has to Offer:

Business Needs of their Customers that their Value-Added Services can Assist:

Decision-Making Process for Hiring:

How will You Follow Up and Ensure Customer Satisfaction?:

What are You Doing to Build Supportive Relationships with Customer?:

## EXERCISE 2

Using the guide above, research your #1 employer target and fill in the relevant information. Over time, you will need to do this in preparation for every interview, even if you interview with a company that is not on your list.

## BACKGROUND CHECKS

Any successful candidate will be required to go through a complete background check. Normally, when you apply to a company or are invited in for an interview, you will be required to fill out a formal application, which is in addition to supplying a resume. The application will require information on your home address; social security number; detailed job experience, including dates, job titles, and salaries; academic record; felony convictions (DWI is a felony in most states); credit information; professional certifications; and any other required information relating to the job.

Included in the application is a legal release form which allows the company to check almost anything related to the qualifications, citizenship, and behavior of the job candidate. This release results in a contract between the candidate and the company, and the candidate certifies that he or she is not lying or misrepresenting anything in his or her background. The release allows for the termination or disqualification of any candidate who lies or misrepresents the information. Many companies will also check social networks, and do a drug test. It is critical not to lie or misrepresent anything in your background. This will result in termination or disqualification.

---

### ACTUAL CASE #1

A graduate school candidate applied to a major TV company for a business-related position. This candidate had done a great job academically and was one of the leaders of the graduating class. The company was very interested in employing the candidate and indicated that they would do a full background check. The company checked social networks and found postings of the candidate in group activities doing drugs and actively engaging in binge drinking. The company dropped the candidate and moved on to another.

---

### ACTUAL CASE #2

A recent college graduate applied to a company for a professional job. The candidate appeared to have good qualifications and the company made an offer contingent upon passing a background check and a drug test. The background check came out OK, but the drug test showed cannabis. The company terminated the candidate.

---

Some common reasons for disqualification as an outcome of a background check include:

- Non-US citizen without proper work permits
- Stolen identity
- Dates of employment and/or education are misrepresented
- Performance feedback from previous employer shows problems
- Academic qualifications don't check
- Poor credit record, particularly for finance or retail jobs
- Felony convictions
- Problematic information on social networking sites
- Failed drug test resulting from using an illegal substance
- Legality in Employment

## LEGAL RAMIFICATIONS OF THE INTERVIEW AND THE HIRING PROCESS

### Illegal Interview Questions

When a company is making decisions on whether to hire or retain individuals, there are a number of factors that the company must NOT consider. The factors include:

- Race
- Ethnicity
- Sex
- Religion
- Age
- Disability
- National origin
- Marital/family status
- Sexual orientation

Companies should tailor their interview questions to avoid soliciting this information. In addition to raising legal issues, asking such questions could make an interview uncomfortable and create an environment where the candidate performs badly. Be mindful not to inadvertently share this information during the interview or in a cover letter!

## Lying on a Resume

Some states have enacted statutes that deem resume fraud a criminal offense; however, these statutes are narrowly applied. In these states it is illegal to utilize a false degree issued by a "diploma mill" to procure employment. "Diploma mills" refer to unaccredited institutions that often hand diplomas to any paying customer. Aside from this narrow prohibition, no US laws criminalize lying on an employment resume. That said, lying or misrepresenting employment or educational history, licensure or expertise, may amount to just-cause for termination.

> **ACTUAL CASE #3**
>
> An individual applying to become president of a software company made multiple misrepresentations on his resume. In addition to lying about his educational credential, he also falsified information regarding his military background and his expertise in Tae Kwon Do. Could an employer consider any of these misrepresentations in terminating an individual?

Yes, all of these could be grounds for termination, depending upon the hiring laws of the state and on whether or not the falsification is considered "material." Materiality depends on the satisfaction of two conditions.

1. The falsification must be firstly related to a requirement for employment.
2. The employer must rely on the falsified information when making the hiring decision.

When such conditions are satisfied, the falsification is deemed material and an employer has just-cause to terminate the employee.

## DISCRIMINATION IN THE WORKPLACE

Federal and state laws, particularly in the last few decades, have attempted to curb discrimination in the workplace. Such laws have addressed the following types of discrimination.

- **SEX DISCRIMINATION.** Sexual discrimination statutes aim to prevent a hostile work environment for all genders and gender identification. Additionally, the Pregnancy Discrimination Act mandated that pregnancy and related conditions be treated like other temporary conditions or illnesses.

- **RELIGIOUS DISCRIMINATION.** An employer must make reasonable accommodations for an employee's religious beliefs, unless doing so would pose an undue hardship.
- **DISABILITY DISCRIMINATION.** Under the Americans with Disabilities Act (ADA), an individual with a disability is someone with: 1) a physical or mental impairment that substantially limits a major life activity, 2) someone with a record of such impairment, or 3) someone who is regarded as having a disability. An individual with a disability is qualified for a job if they possess the skill, experience, education, and other job-related requirements for the position. Such an individual must be able to perform the key functions of that position, with or without reasonable accommodation. An employer is required to make reasonable accommodations for a qualified individual with a disability unless doing so would pose undue hardship. Undue hardship amounts to a significant difficulty or expense for an employer, with consideration of the business' resources and size.
- **AGE DISCRIMINATION.** An employer is prevented from imposing age specifications, preferences, or limits for employment unless age amounts to a BFOQ. Additionally, statues protect older employees from being denied benefits.
- **EQUAL WAGES.** The law seeks to ensure that men and women are paid equally when performing work of similar effort, skill, and responsibility under similar work conditions.

# BE INTENTIONAL

- ALWAYS THANK THE ADMINISTRATIVE ASSISTANT AND/OR RECEPTIONIST WHEN YOU LEAVE FOLLOWING AN ON-SITE INTERVIEW.
- GET A HAIRCUT OR SHAVE IF YOU FEEL YOU PROBABLY SHOULD.
- IF YOU WONDER IF A CERTAIN OUTFIT IS APPROPRIATE FOR AN INTERVIEW, CHANGE INTO SOMETHING THAT YOU KNOW, FOR CERTAIN, IS.
- READ A BOOK ON HOW TO DRESS SUCCESSFULLY.
- PROVIDE THE LITTLE TOUCHES, LIKE A HAND WRITTEN THANK-YOU NOTE.
- LEARN SOMETHING ABOUT THE AREA OR TOWN BEFORE YOU INTERVIEW IN A NEW PLACE.

# CHAPTER 14

# Assessing the Offers and Negotiating the Deal

## OUTCOME:

**I WILL KNOW HOW TO ASSESS ALL JOB OFFERS I HAVE RECEIVED AND NEGOTIATE THE BEST DEAL POSSIBLE FOR ME AND FOR MY FUTURE.**

## JOB OFFERS

Once all interviews are complete, and background checks have been finalized, a successful candidate will receive a job offer, which is, of course, the objective and goal from the onset. Typically, the initial offer will be verbal, generally followed by a letter or email that outlines the specifics of the offer. The initial offer may include:

- Starting salary
- Bonus or incentive eligibility, if applicable
- Job title
- Starting date of employment
- Probationary periods of job
- Location of work assignment and where and who to report to
- Outline of any relocation assistance
- Start date of benefit coverage
- Any special issues concerning the job

The verbal offer is usually followed by a written offer that outlines all of the provisions of the job situation in more detail.

This will/should include:

- Copy of the job description
- Copies of benefit plans
- Rules and regulations that apply to the job
- Company business and policy information
- Other material related to the company and the job

The written offer may also include a request for additional information from the candidate such as a birth certificate, driver's license, social security card, proof of military service, and/or any other information used in the company's verification process. Some companies will collect pieces of this information during the final interview phase, but be prepared to provide additional documentation as requested, either at the time of acceptance or when you begin work. Also, please note the offer letter will require that you return a copy of the letter to the company with your signature of acceptance. This results in your first contractual agreement with the company.

**Negotiating the Job Offer**

The opportunity to negotiate the job offer happens after the verbal offer, and this is the only chance you'll get so you need to be prepared. Regardless of the quality of the offer, and your intention to accept or decline it, you should always negotiate time to "consider" the offer. At a minimum you should request 24-48 hours. If, after you have considered the offer, you determine that all provisions are satisfactory, you should contact the company within the time allowed and accept the position, and thank the individual who extended the offer both verbally and with a written reply. However, if for some reason the offer doesn't meet your expectations, you have an opportunity to engage in "respectful negotiations."

Setting the stage for respectful negotiations begins with a heartfelt thank you when you receive the verbal offer, along with a request for time to review the verbal and written offers. Most companies will give you a week or two of extension to finalize your acceptance or rejection of the job offer. After that they will press you for an answer. Employers recognize that if a candidate does not accept immediately there may be some issues or problems with the offer. They may also suspect that the candidate has other offer(s) to consider.

Various issues can trigger a candidate's desire to negotiate. These include, but are not limited to, the following:

- Offer salary is too low. In a collegiate setting, an office of career management will have a good picture of the market and the average salaries for different types of graduates. Additionally, various websites like salary.com can guide you in determining what is fair market value.
- The candidate needs time to consider other offers, some of which may be coming later.
- The candidate has related job experience that isn't being recognized in the offer.
- The job involves relocation, and there is no relocation assistance.
- The job involves relocation to a major market that has significantly higher living costs.
- Geographical limitations of the job present problems.
- Requirements of a probationary period had not been previously discussed.
- Job requirements include unanticipated travel.
- Candidate has a valid conflict with the start date (wedding planned, summer military duty, or something else very important).
- There may be other important issues in the offer that were not previously discussed.

Please take note of the following unacceptable reasons to negotiate:
- Need the summer off to go on vacation after graduating
- Not enough vacation time from the company
- Work hours appear to be too long
- Job duties are too difficult

The most common reason for negotiating an offer centers on the salary and/or the need for time to consider another offer(s). Keep in mind that the employer has made an offer to you, has probably completed a full background check, and has already determined that they want you to work in their company. At this point, you have the leverage and, if you need to, this is the time for you to have a respectful negotiation.

To be fully prepared for this, you should do your homework. If the issue is salary, gather the resources that will support your request for a higher salary. Talk to your office of career management and/or use appropriate internet resources to determine appropriate salary ranges for the position and the area. Look online at the rates for college graduates in markets similar to where you will be working. (Keep in mind that if you have more experience than the average graduate, you have a basis to ask for higher salary consideration). The rates are higher in the major cities, perhaps by as much as 10% to 30%. Regardless of the issue, you must do your homework and get the facts before you negotiate.

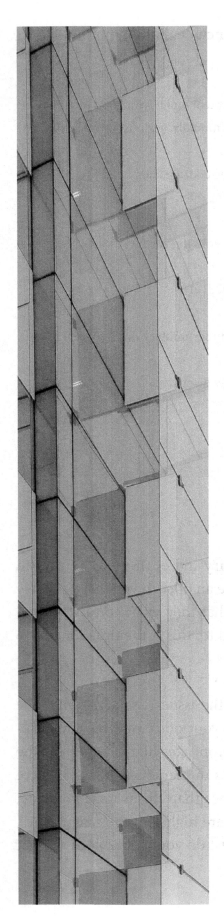

Generally, when you are ready to negotiate, you contact the individual who made the offer to you in the first place. Have a fact-based conversation that will politely demonstrate you have done your homework. The specifics should indicate that the reasons you are asking for additional consideration are valid. You really have nothing to lose, and the worst thing that could happen is the company will not make a change in your terms and conditions of employment.

### Thinking Like the Employer

In conclusion, let's take a minute to "think like the employer" which will provide you with a framework as you head into the negotiations. Remember that employers have a lot to consider when a candidate asks for more money. Organizations that hire college graduates are generally very aware of the salaries being offered to graduates because they share the information with each other and talk to the various career offices. They have an excellent understanding of the market and make their offers based on that knowledge.

One key issue has to do with the college graduates they hired last year. Usually larger employers will hire numerous college graduates each year and they typically bring them in at a similar salary level. For example, imagine that a major company brought in several accounting graduates last year at $58,000. Each of them received a cost of living increase, so the average salary of the group is $61,000. To maintain a level of fairness, the employer will not bring in new hires at salaries that get too close to $61,000. The maximum they are likely to offer is $55,000 to $58,000, unless a candidate has exceptional experience or is in the top 5% of the class. You must know this information, and consider all of the potential ramifications as you begin the negotiating process.

With this in mind, knowing some of the top candidates are going to require additional monetary incentives, employers will sometimes have flexibility with up-front bonuses or one-time payments for something specific. It is much easier for a company to make an up-front one-time payment that increases a base salary offer.

## CASE: A TYPICAL SALARY NEGOTIATION

A graduating business student in Tennessee had a verbal offer of $55,000 from a company in Chicago that appeared to be a little low. The offer did not include any relocation assistance. The human resources representative extended the offer via telephone. The job candidate thanked the HR officer and told him that she loved the company and all the people she met there, but asked for a week to review the offer. The candidate was concerned that the dollar offer might not be enough to rent an apartment and help her move to Chicago. She did her homework and found that Chicago had a higher cost of living and apartments were 20% higher than Knoxville, Tennessee. She also estimated her moving costs, and felt that she needed at least $7,000 a year more in salary. At the end of the week, she called the human resources representative for the company and told him she was very interested in the company, but needed some consideration for the financial issues that she researched. She had a respectful conversation by outlining the facts. The company told her that they could not be flexible on base salary because it would impact other recent graduates they were hiring as well as the graduates they hired last year. They said they could offer her an upfront bonus of $10,000 in recognition of the fact she was moving from Knoxville to Chicago. The candidate accepted the bonus and moved to Chicago.

One last reminder, if you want to negotiate with an employer, it must be done respectfully. You must do your homework and present a polite case, with a factual backup. You can't negotiate for more just because you want more. Also, remember that the company has offered you a job. They want you! Consequently, the only downside is that they say no to your request. There is no harm in trying if you have a legitimate case.

# BE INTENTIONAL

- BE OPEN AND CANDID ABOUT THE COMPENSATION SYSTEM.
- ASK FOR WHAT YOU WANT AS LONG AS YOUR CASE IS VALID.
- TAKE RISKS.

# CHAPTER 15

# Transitioning to the Job

OUTCOME:

## I WILL KNOW THE MAIN THINGS I NEED TO CONSIDER AS I TRANSITION INTO A NEW JOB.

Congratulations on successfully completing your search! As you begin this new journey, it is important to keep in mind that the "interview" continues, at least for a while. As you are adjusting to the new job, remember that you ended up at this place because someone or a group of individuals gave you an opportunity and took a risk on you. Their examination of you and your abilities will continue for quite some time.

As you start your new job, you are most likely on a spoken or an unspoken probation or trial period for three to six months. If you are starting an internship, please be aware that the entire internship is a continuation of the interview both for you and for them. You now have the opportunity to prove you have what it takes to do the job you have been hired to do, and that you have all the skills and competencies you told them about in the interview process.

To fully maximize this probationary period or internship experience, please remember that you will be watched very closely so that the following can be fully assessed:

- Your work ethic
- Your eagerness and curiosity to learn
- Your meeting or exceeding expectations (standards)
- Your ability to work with others

Simultaneously, it will be crucial that you begin to understand your direct supervisor or manager. This is important, obviously, because you need to know what this individual expects and learn about his or her management style. Equally important, however, is an understanding of how well this individual is likely to meet your needs, and how they may cause you stress. Remember that rare is the manager who will meet all of your needs or, in some cases, even care that you have them. You must understand these needs, ask for what you need, or recognize that, at times, they won't be met, depending upon the situation and the manager. Obviously, for all of us, there are situations that are simply intolerable. Hopefully you have vetted all of your opportunities and are in a job that closely aligns with your overall needs and strengths.

Let's revisit your Birkman results in light of what you need from others, including your new manager. We will look at two different reports to gain a fuller understanding of what you need individually from your manager, specifically in communication, and what you need in general terms to stay appropriately motivated.

**Please locate and read, "How to Talk to Him/Her" and the report titled "Motivating for Best Performance."**

While we won't do a formal exercise here, please read these carefully and refer back to them as needed throughout the first few months of your new job or at the conclusion of your internship. It is inevitable that some of these needs will not be met on a consistent basis, but knowing what they are can help you avoid derailing reactions.

Remember, now that you are employed your primary customer is your new boss, as well as your co-workers. Your immediate supervisor deserves your loyalty, commitment, and desire to learn and move the entire organization forward. In this context, your most valuable asset is your credibility or integrity. Don't do anything that would jeopardize or lessen either.

- Be on time. (10 minutes before the appointed time.)
- Perform your responsibilities, duties, and administrative requirements.
- Work hard and be ready to spend time on what is necessary. (Be engaged in your job.)
- Learn.
- Do what you said you would do when you were interviewed.

Finally, it will be your responsibility, and yours alone, to determine what aspects of your Birkman results you share with your new manager. The results of your answers to The Birkman Method® have pointed out many of your strengths and weaknesses that you and your manager can build upon, but you will need to be savvy in determining what to share and when to share it.

That said, even if you choose to share none of your results directly with your supervisor, you need to spend some time reviewing your results in light of your performance at work, and in light of your potential reaction to the stress that will inevitably come with a new position. In addition, there are several other reports included in your Birkman packet that you are encouraged to review. The more you know about your strengths, needs, and interests, the better prepared you will be to see success in this phase of your career.

# CONCLUDING THOUGHTS

AS YOU BEGIN THIS NEW JOURNEY, AND AS YOU FACE THE INEVITABLE CHALLENGES THAT WILL ARISE, THE MOST IMPORTANT THING TO UNDERSTAND IS YOURSELF. BEING DEEPLY GROUNDED IN AN UNDERSTANDING OF WHO YOU ARE, WHAT YOU ENJOY, WHAT YOUR STRENGTHS ARE, AND WHAT YOU NEED WILL CARRY YOU FARTHER DOWN THE PATH TO SUCCESS THAN ANYTHING ELSE. NEVER QUIT LEARNING AND NEVER STOP LOOKING INWARD FOR THE ANSWERS.

**GOOD LUCK!**

# LEVERAGING SOCIAL MEDIA

BY DR. FELIPE THOMAZ

In all likelihood you are already familiar with social media in your day-to-day life. Platforms like Facebook, Twitter, LinkedIn, Instagram, Pinterest, Snapchat and others have significantly changed the way people connect, communicate, and share many aspects of their daily lives. Similarly, social media is changing the way almost all companies communicate with their customers. Just like most people, these companies maintain a presence in a variety of platforms where they too can connect, communicate and share. Unsurprisingly, given the mix of everyday life, people, and companies, this environment offers as many opportunities as it does traps for potential job seekers. As such, understanding how to manage it appropriately should prove to be quite beneficial during many phases of your job search.

Thankfully, much of what you've already covered will help you in successfully navigating your process in a social media space, and you can begin to turn all of these social connections and discussions to your advantage. Naturally, as a broad force in our society, social media will impact several components of the "Pathway to Getting the Right Job" that you are following. We'll discuss each of these in turn.

## PERCEPTION IS REALITY

Chapter 3 of this book introduced the notion that your actions, and attitudes reflect some information about yourself, and that others use this potentially limited information to create a representation of who you are as a professional. This representation is your personal brand, and you are the "product" being sold in the job search process. Like any product, your brand is a huge differentiator, and likely the reason you would get a job instead of someone else even when both of you have all of the same qualifications. Strong brands not only drive choice, but also value, meaning that a strong personal brand could also lead to higher pay. All the more reason to be mindful of your brand!

So, how does social media affect your personal brand? Like most things related to social media, it multiplies in size and scope. If previously you were worried about what you said to someone, or how you acted during an interview, or how you dressed/presented yourself in a more social occasion, consider now the amount of information potentially available about you online Consider your status updates and pictures on Facebook, tweets to friends, books and topics you noted as interesting, etc. Consider information that you make available about yourself, as well as the things your friends make available. There is simply a potentially enormous amount of information impacting your brand. Most of it related to things that would never come up in a professional/interview setting.

It is true that there is an ongoing discussion about the ethics of f iiiis using this personal informtion in hiring decisions, but there are largely no laws describing what can and cannot be used, only guidelines. Additionally, remember that recruiters are humans too, and are doing their best to find the best person for the job...it can be hard to avoid looking up your candidates online In fact, more than 60% of companies check their candidates' online profiles, and this number is likely to continue to grow. So, the best approach is to actively manage what others can see about you. You will have a "digital footprint" simply by virtue of existing and interacting online, so you might as well make it work for you.

Some things that are not discussed in applications or interviews will be obvious from your digital presence: gender, race, ethnicity, age, any disabilities, etc. Now, as you know, these items are legally protected, and are not to influence hiring decisions. However, other items have cost applicants' their job opportunities: inappropriate photographs, bad attitudes towards previous employers and fellow employees, discriminatory comments, general information about drug use/abuse and or excessive alcohol use. It is also not uncommon for recruiters to gauge applicants' communication skills by how they express themselves online, nor is it unlikely for them to confirm prior experience and/or qualifications through social media. Even if many of these items are not officially entered into the firm's decision criteria, there is still the "I can't un-see this picture, or that comment" which could damage your brand, and with it your chances at landing a specific job. It is possible for recruiters to simply assume that you are "not a good fit for the company's culture" and dismiss an application at that point.

However, there is a fairly straightforward solution. Start by making your social media accounts private (if able), thus limiting what information is visible outside of your group of friends/family. Additionally, manage your list of friends carefully. Privacy settings are of little use to you if you add the recruiter/interviewer to your friends list after your meeting. At no point can recruiters request your social media passwords (this is one instance where several states have passed a law protecting individuals against social media intrusion).

For those services where privacy is not an option, consider managing your content. Pay attention to what you say, what you post, and what others post about you. This is tremendous important step as we move away from a "hiding the bad/inappropriate stuff" strategy to using social media to your advantage as a brand-building tool. How?

Make sure that the information you are providing in your public social media accounts is consistent with what you present in person, and that both of these are consistent with the professional brand/impression you are attempting to create. This is easily done via:

- Engaging in online conversation. There are several groups online that are specific for industry-related or trade-related discussions. Join the conversation to demonstrate knowledge, expertise, and interest.
- Sharing Content. Engage with experts in your field and share what they have to say with others. Share interesting/relevant articles.
- Creating Content. Contribute your own insights via blog posts, articles, etc.

Perception is truly reality, and social media does provide you with tools to manage perception, your image, your personal brand, and your value to potential employers. Creating a strong brand as suggested above might not only assist with current job applications, but might also translate into new opportunities as more managers and recruiters come across your content.

## PREPARING FOR THE INTERVIEW

How else can we take advantage of social media in our job search process? One fairly valuable initiative takes place during your preparation for an interview. You should already be engaging in some "due diligence" ahead of your interview by researching the position and seeking to understand the company, its culture, and employees ahead of your first meeting. You can extend this process by flipping the process we just discussed back onto the firm and doing your own social listening, or using their digital footprint to get more information and attempt to gauge what they value most, or on how you should position yourself to increase your chances of getting their offer.

By investing some time and effort you can go through a firm's social media presence (LinkedIn, Facebook, Twitter, Instagram, etc) and take note of their updates, what they choose to share or comment on, the extent of their activity in general (do they post at all, a little, or a lot). Take note of who they engage with, as well as what they share from other sources. At the very least, this research should give you an idea of how they compete in the marketplace and what sort of value they see themselves as providing to their customers. At this point you should ask yourself how you can contribute to this strategy, and what value you bring to the company — this will be something you'll want to get across during your interview since you are trying to place yourself as the best "product" for them.

With a little more digging you might find other important pieces of information that can be used during the interview. Maybe the company is expanding into a new location, or into a new country. Maybe the president of the company made a recent announcement or statement that impacts the position for which you are interviewing. All of these examples lead to great questions during the interview. For instance, "How will the expansion into XYZ impact my potential duties?" or "With the company moving into XYZ, are there opportunities for me to engage/interact with those managers and learn from their experiences" or "Considering Mr. CEO's statement last Tuesday, how do you see the growth of the division we're talking about...", etc.

In fact, with enough time and energy, you can employ this approach for the firm's competitor's as well to get a more complete understanding of everything the firm is facing. Whether you choose to engage in social listening or not and how much depends on the type of position you are interviewing for, and who you expect to be interviewing with, since some questions might be appropriate for managers with more intimate knowledge of day-to-day operations. However, the advantage in the approach is clear: demonstrate knowledge about the company, demonstrate interest, and further set yourself apart from other candidates.

Additional social listening can happen in professional social platforms like LinkedIn, where you can turn your focus away from the firm itself and towards its current and former employees. You can use the information contained here to understand the background of their employees or to gauge the common skillsets that lead to, or arise from, employment in the firm. Does it look like a good match from your perspective? Are you bringing something novel or unique to this position? You certainly would want to bring up any of these points in an interview to further highlight the value you potentially bring to the company. Along similar lines, you can attempt to determine an average tenure time for employees in that company. There's a good chance that a company that does not keep employees for more than a few months at a time has some internal/culture problems that are not immediately visible from outside or from asking questions during the interview process. This sort of information could be invaluable to you when choosing the right job offer.

## NETWORKING

Chapter 8 already introduced you to the networking concept (or at least reminded you of its incredible importance). In our discussion on using social media to your advantage, we also covered many things that are intimately related to networking, like connecting to industry leaders, and sharing content (obviously, you need an audience to receive this content). Your online contacts from Facebook and LinkedIn, or anywhere else, could be the ones supporting your application to a new job, or the ones to let you know about a new opportunity in the first place. Having a strong network of supporters is incredibly valuable in any career, and even more so when looking for the next/best opportunity.

Aside from following the suggestions already discussed in this and earlier chapters, managing your online network has one additional important caveat: your are not "collecting friends." Many people get lost in the numbers game, much in the same way that companies fight over have the largest number of fans on Facebook, but you have to ask yourself this question: what is the value of adding one additional name to your contacts list if they never see/hear anything from you? It should be clear that being a silent member of your own network is not going to get you results, and that having the most number of connections is fairly meaningless compared to having a few people that are engaged with and supportive of you.

In the earlier discussion on networks, it was made fairly clear that these connections should be leads to future conversations. The same is true in social media, but that barrier associated with these conversations is much smaller. It was already suggested that you should join the conversation to demonstrate your interest and expertise. Engage further, share their content, comment on it, congratulate them on achievements, etc. It does not to be excessive, or invasive, but you should make an honest effort to enter the conversation, to remain relevant, visible and engaged.

The key point to remember is that having lots of contacts is helpful but not sufficient for success. Your success will depend on how you use your network, and that you'll need to **add** value to it by contributing conversation, content, and insight before you can **extract** value from it in the foim of job opportunities and referrals. Building the network and your value to it does not happen over-night. It actually takes a significant amount of time and effort, but you'll be able to reap benefits from it now, and likely for a very long time afterwards.

# APPENDIX

# OVERVIEW OF THE 12 LEVELS OF THE PATHWAY TO SUCCESS

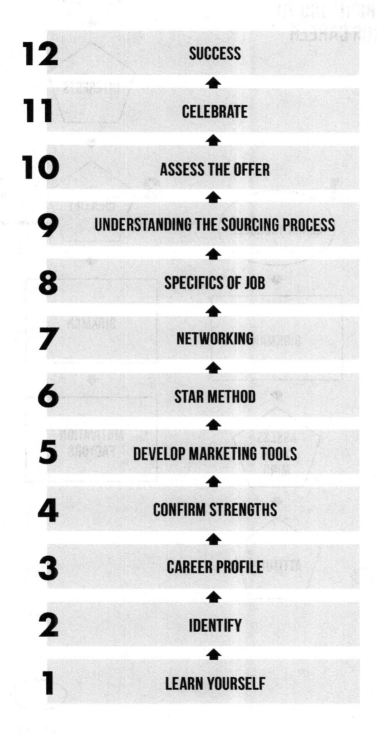

| 12 | SUCCESS |
| 11 | CELEBRATE |
| 10 | ASSESS THE OFFER |
| 9 | UNDERSTANDING THE SOURCING PROCESS |
| 8 | SPECIFICS OF JOB |
| 7 | NETWORKING |
| 6 | STAR METHOD |
| 5 | DEVELOP MARKETING TOOLS |
| 4 | CONFIRM STRENGTHS |
| 3 | CAREER PROFILE |
| 2 | IDENTIFY |
| 1 | LEARN YOURSELF |

IF YOU KNOW WHAT YOU WANT, EXPECT TO GET IT, HAVE
DONE ENOUGH FOR THE OTHER PERSON, ASK FOR WHAT YOU WANT,
AND FOLLOW A DENITE PLAN, YOU WILL GET WHAT YOU WANT.

# PATHWAY

**GETTING THE RIGHT JOB TO DEVELOP YOUR CAREER**

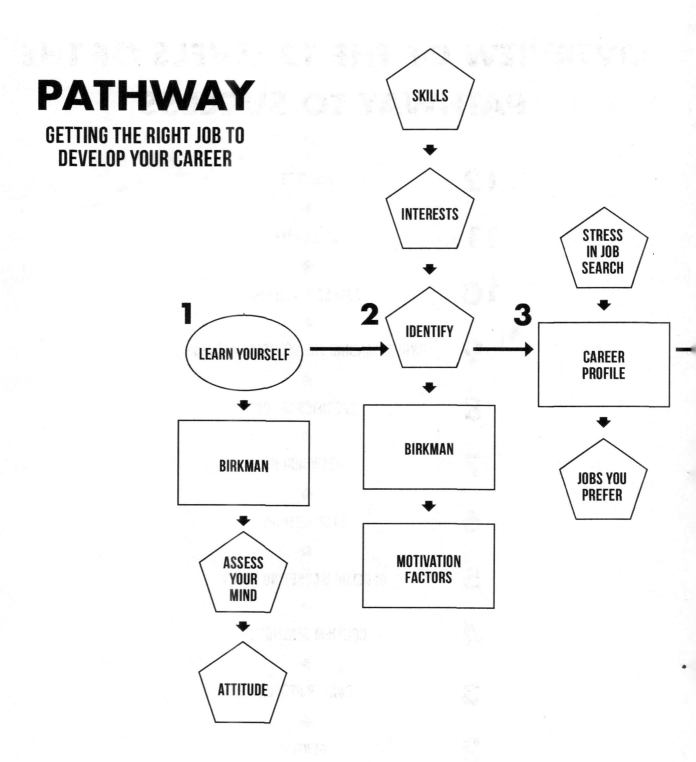

**SKILLS**

**INTERESTS**

**1** LEARN YOURSELF

**2** IDENTIFY

**3** CAREER PROFILE

STRESS IN JOB SEARCH

BIRKMAN

BIRKMAN

ASSESS YOUR MIND

MOTIVATION FACTORS

JOBS YOU PREFER

ATTITUDE

BEGINNING/END

DECISION MAKING

ACTION STEP

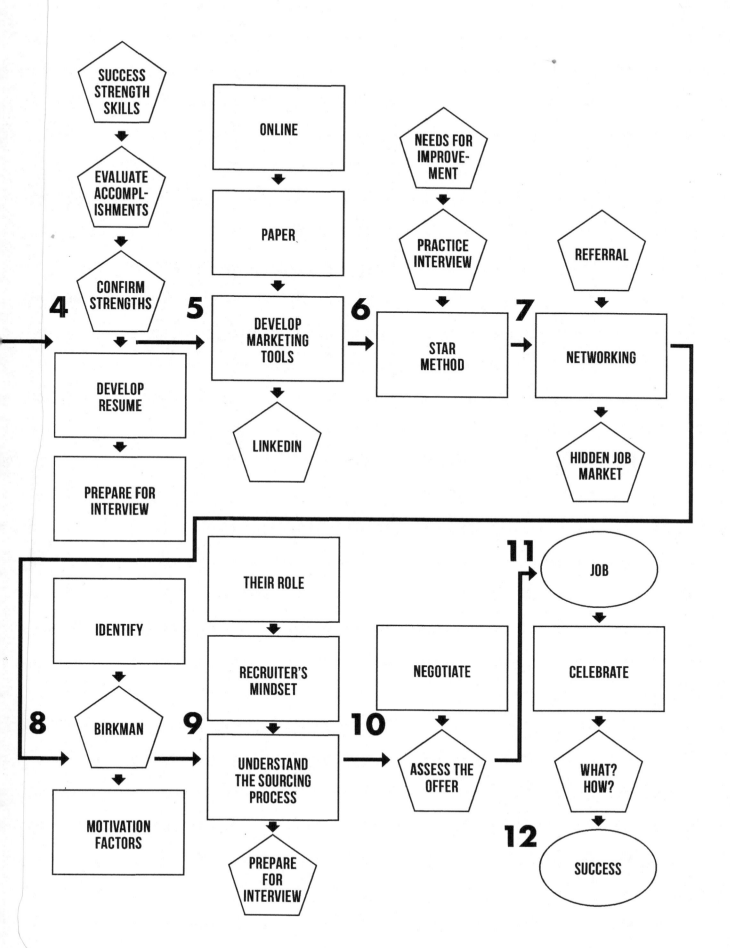